Literate Days:

Reading and Writing with Preschool and Primary Children

Gretchen Owocki

*first*hand

HEINEMANN

Photographer: David Stirling
DVD Producers: Kevin Carlson and Pip Clews
Editor: Pip Clews
Location production services: D2 Productions

The author and publisher wish to thank those who have generously given permission to reprint borrowed materials.

Post-it® is a registered trademark of the 3M Company.

Play-Doh® is a registered trademark of Hasbro, Inc.

TV Guide® is a registered trademark of TV Guide Magazine Group, Inc.

Cheerios® is a registered trademark of General Mills, Inc.

Batman® is a registered trademark of DC Comics.

Wikki Stix® is registered trademark of Omnicor, Inc.

*first*hand

An imprint of Heinemann
A division of Reed Elsevier Inc.
361 Hanover Street
Portsmouth, NH 03801-3912
www.firsthand.heinemann.com

Offices and agents throughout the world

Library of Congress Catalog-in-Publication Data
CIP data on file with the Library of Congress

ISBN-10: 0-325-01208-3
ISBN-13: 978-0-325-01208-7

Printed in the United States of America on acid-free paper

11 10 09 08 07 ML 1 2 3 4 5 6

Table of Contents

Literate Days:

Snapshot of a Literate Day

To get a feel for what children in a Literate Days classroom experience on a daily basis, read this snapshot.

Imagine stepping into an early childhood classroom one morning as the children are just arriving for the day. The entry area is a flurry of backpacks coming off; jackets hung and flung; cheerful greetings among friends; and an eager audience jostling to see the new cast on the broken wrist of a proud classmate. The children's activity makes it clear that there is a sense of community here. They greet one another by name; express awe at the cast and sympathy about the wrist; and help others remember to check their backpacks for books and papers they will need for the day.

One of the first things that you notice as you make your way through this action is a child-sized table used for signing in and recording lunch preferences. The table serves as a sort of border, physical and psychological, between the robust activity of the entry area and the more composed area of the classroom. Right now the table holds a few pads of 3x5 Post-it notes. A small child stands at the table, with her father at her side. (He is visiting for the morning.) Chin held high, she straightens the pink Post-it she has chosen and lines it up evenly with the table's edge. She selects a purple marker and carefully removes the cap. She touches her finger to the tip of the marker to be sure that the ink is good. And then she glances at her dad to see that he is paying attention. This child appears to sense that she is doing something important, and she is. She's signing her own name.

1

Signing in is a way for this child to record her presence, and to begin the official business of the school day. When she signs her name, she knows that she is to begin to focus on school routines and school learning. Her teacher has talked with the children about this: "When you sign in here, it lets me know you are here, but it also means you are ready to come in and think about learning. That's why you're here, you know—to learn how to do new things and to learn all about the world we live in."

The sign-in sheet is just one example of **the print all over this classroom;** not *just* print, but print that is *created* by children, and *used* by children. For example, many children are already looking at books in the classroom library. Some are choosing books that the class has created. The books in the library are labeled according to author, topic, and genre because the teacher wants the children to

develop tastes and preferences for book types and topics—and a conscious awareness of these. She knows that motivation to read is supported by children being connected with just the right content. A checkout sheet is available for children who wish to take books home. There's a huge snack calendar (hung at children's eye level) that the children can actually read because it has labels from real food packages taped to it. Someone has cut out labels from graham crackers, apples, Cheerios, trail mix, and muffin packages so that the *children*

can read for themselves what's for snack this week. On the wall, there hangs a schedule that helps children know which learning centers they may attend on this day.

What you're seeing in this classroom is a setting in which children are *involved* in literacy as a regular part of daily life. As you can imagine, the teacher's planning and teaching play an important role in this process. Because she believes that children learn a great deal about reading and writing when they use print in real contexts, she makes it a goal to let children do real-life activities, every day, *as* she works to teach essential skills and strategies.

A key part of her efforts involves explicitly **familiarizing the children with the discourses** they need for being successful with classroom literacy practices. For example, her teaching often uses language such as this: "When you use the classroom library, here's what you are expected to do." "In case you ever want to know what we are doing on a day, let me show you how to check our daily schedule." "When you don't know how to spell a word, please do this." The more familiar children become with the patterns of and expectations for varied literacy practices in a classroom, the more independent and successful they can become. Effective teaching mixes **immersion in the community of practice** with **scaffolding** that focuses learners on key patterns of that practice; patterns that help children learn to act, work, and think in specific ways (Gee 2000). So as you read on, look for lots of immersion in reading and writing, with lots of explicit

Name Avery   Date 10-23-06

I was helping my
sister ciing to
to sowd uot
X werds. it was fun.

instruction taking place as the reading and writing occur. The lessons in *Literate Days* are built on the principle that children learn best when their instruction occurs during meaningful literacy events.

Not long after the children enter the classroom and sign in, the teacher catches their attention by initiating the **singing** of a familiar song. The children have been taught that this is their signal to convene on the rug. The *Lessons from Literate Days* DVD includes a section featuring the many songs one preschool teacher uses to teach throughout the day. When the song ends, the children quickly greet the child to their left and to their right with a simple, "Hello, _____. How are you?" (a pattern the teacher has taught). Next is a time for **conversation.** The teacher asks, "Who has something remarkable to share?" and the child with the new cast reports in depth on how she broke her wrist. The teacher then leads the children in a quick review of the **calendar.** Long calendar reviews can be excruciatingly tedious, but this approach is quick and serves a purpose, and respects the true function of a calendar as well as what is meaningful to the students: the teacher shows the children how she locates the day and date. In the appropriate box on the calendar, she has written special events for the day. It is here that the class learns whether they will have music or physical education class, a special visitor, a special project, or a birthday to celebrate. What is most important about the first few minutes of this morning is that already, all of the children have been greeted by name, and all have a general picture of what to expect for the day. They are settling in, and the environment is warm and predictable.

After the greeting and conversation, this first **circle meeting** of the morning becomes highly focused. The teacher's goal every morning is to support children's literacy development through two kinds of whole-class reading experiences. She starts with **shared reading.** Here, she leads the children in the reading of a large-print poem, rhyme, or big book (sometimes they read the same piece for several days), and provides contextualized strategy and skill instruction before and after the reading. Her specific focus is on teaching children to use strategies to process (or decode) text. She uses this opportunity to teach anything from how to use context to determine an unknown word to how to analyze a word by looking at its parts; she might use the moment to discuss an author's interesting word choices or to highlight the word families that are repeated several times in the text. What she teaches is dependent on what she has observed many of her students to need; she tailors her instruction to connect with needs that she has observed through kidwatching. Throughout *Literate Days* you will find many kidwatching tools designed to help you fine tune and tailor your instruction.

Literature selection for shared reading is important. The teacher chooses short, predictable-language pieces that are fun to read and repeat — the kind you can't get out of your own mind and hear kids repeating all day — or she chooses text that has a predictable, often repetitive story line, so that readers have lots of clues to what the words on the page say. Book 1 contains literature recommendations for shared reading.

The **read-aloud** is next. The teacher again puts great effort into selecting the text. She consciously works to choose read-aloud literature that will be engaging to her students; that will raise questions in their minds; and that they will *want* to grapple with and talk about. This is important because it is the time of day that she focuses most intensely on teaching comprehension strategies. If we want to teach comprehension strategies well, we must ensure that children *want* to comprehend, and want to *work* to comprehend. Sometimes the read-aloud text relates to the social studies or science explorations that the children are currently engaged with; other times the text is chosen just for the sake of reading a good piece of literature. At all times, the focus is on helping students to develop as literate individuals and to develop their world knowledge. The teaching of comprehension strategies fosters both of these processes: as the teacher and students explore the text, she teaches them to focus on meaning and encourages them to "Picture this in your mind;" "Rethink this part—it seems really important;" "Let's think through your question as a class—I'm not sure I understand either!"; "Think about what is new to you here—what did you learn?" The focus on **thinking like a reader** is explicit. "This is what readers do," she tells them. "They think a lot about what they have read and they work to understand it."

After the circle meeting, the daily **reading workshop** begins. This is when students are assigned either to take some more time to respond to the literature just read (through an activity back at their tables) or to engage in partner reading. On this particular day, the students are sent off to respond further to *Traction Man* (Mini Grey), a book that has generated much interest and some healthy confusion among the group. Traction Man is a superhero figure that comes to life in the imagination of the boy character who plays with him. (The boy is just pretending, right?) The children are back at their tables, talking and drawing about the ways they play and imagine with their own things at home, and trying out some of the creative techniques used by the author/illustrator — all in an attempt to develop better insight into this unique story. The class is going to read the book again tomorrow and talk about it some more — because it's clear to the teacher that they are simply *not* finished pursuing meaning from this book.

As the children finish their responses to the literature (or, on other days, their partner reading), they move into learning centers — on their own time. If they want to continue with their partner reading when center time begins, they do! If they want to continue working with ideas from the book the teacher has read aloud, they do! The teacher sees productive learning activity as activity that engages. She does not interrupt children who are engaged in learning, unless she has to. Sometimes, the best learning is the kind that is unplanned by the teacher and initiated by the students because of a genuine curiosity, question, or interest. Watching for unexpected learning moments — and letting them live — is part of having faith

in children as learners, and every theory of learning ever written tells us that we can do just that: we can have faith in children as learners.

Five **core learning centers** are used throughout the year in this classroom. Every day, the children have access to the classroom library, the sociodramatic play center (in which literacy materials are incorporated), the easel center (for shared reading and writing), the writing table, and the listening center. Other typical centers in this classroom involve retelling with props, reading from a set of content area book bins, playing word and letter games, engaging in an experiment or activity related to science or social studies, and making art. Book 1 contains many ideas for planning and setting up centers.

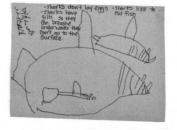

The children work and move from center to center with a noticeable independence. For the first months of the school year, the teacher spent a great deal of time providing explicit instruction about expectations for literacy practices — *as* the children were immersed in these practices. She helped them explore and talk through the kinds of work they were capable of doing; she taught them new ways to collaborate with one another; she showed them what to do to effectively set up, participate in, and complete their learning center activities. It was worth it to build management right into her instruction because she now has long stretches of time for in-depth instruction — with few interruptions. This teacher spends some of center time working with the children in the centers, and some of the time is spent working with small groups of readers.

The reading workshop ends with a **closure** period for children to share ideas, processes, and products created during the morning. On this day, all students are asked to bring something to share with a peer, and they are given a few minutes to talk about their morning activity. The teacher then asks for any volunteers to "share something remarkable from workshop time." A small boy who rarely talks at school and has never volunteered to share with the group has been inspired by *Traction Man*. He raises his hand. When he is called on, he seems to change his mind about sharing. He sits silently, uncomfortably, holding his drawing against his body so that it cannot be seen. A rather long silence ensues. "Show us your picture?" the teacher suggests. The boy shakes his head almost imperceptibly but then suddenly holds up his paper, turning his head to the side to avoid any eye-contact with the class. The drawing (it originally showed a nice black-crayon drawing of Batman) has had so much action taken on it that any of the original lines are difficult to see, and the final product is a criss-cross of black lines (drawn to represent Batman's action). The children look from the paper to the teacher's face, almost as if for a cue about how to handle this unexpected situation. The teacher gazes at the drawing with a look of appreciation. She understands children's development — and she has kid-watched all morning — so she knows just what to say. "Wow," she quite softly states. "I can see that many remarkable things happened as you worked on that drawing." The boy looks at her with a combination of surprise and gratefulness on his face. Another boy, who sat near the child as he was working, asks him, "What did you have Batman doing?"

After a break that involves outdoor play and a snack, **writing workshop** begins. (It should be noted that during the break, several children offered to help the child with the cast manage her jacket and her snack; the teacher asked if she could hang the blackened Batman picture on the easel and the Batman illustrator declared, "I'm going to write more about that. Some kids wanted to know things"; and the visiting father was invited to come back at any time.)

The teacher opens the writing workshop with a whole-class **minilesson** that relates to the students' general needs *at present.* Typically, even though their topics differ, the students are all writing within the same genre. So, the minilesson may focus on something related to genre, such as writing a good opener for a nonfiction piece; developing a character in a story; labeling the parts of a drawing created as part of a science inquiry; or adding conversation to a drawing of an imaginary character (such as Batman). Or the lessons may be more oriented toward specific writing strategies and skills such as generating invented spellings, looking for unconventional spellings in a finished piece, using the spelling resources in the classroom, or thinking about punctuation. As the students write, the teacher **conferences** with individuals, and sometimes with small groups. Here, she **individualizes** and **differentiates** her instruction. If students need help with getting words on paper, she provides it. If students need help generating ideas, she provides it. Within the workshop, each child works from a place of strength, and receives support tailored to specific needs.

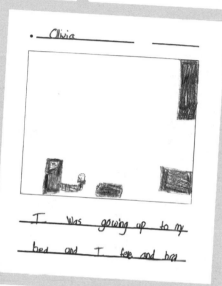

The rest of the day provides opportunities for more specific work in the **content areas** of math, science, and social studies, but **integration** is always a part of what happens in this classroom. Morning read-alouds often make use of texts related to science and social studies inquiries. What's especially beneficial here is that those texts are not just read once through; they are also *studied*— and studied again when children express a special interest in them. Writing workshop pieces often focus on content-area topics. And centers often include content-area explorations and content-area books to view and/or read. When children read and write for real purposes in a classroom, integration is a natural byproduct.

The classroom described here provides just one example of what a "literate days" classroom looks like. Because of different teachers, children, settings, and curricula, such classrooms look vastly different in many ways. What is the same is that children are immersed in a community that blends real-life reading and writing with explicit, well-tailored, sensitive instruction.

Literate Days:
Organization and Content

Literate Days is a curriculum resource for preschool, kindergarten, and first-grade teachers looking to enrich and broaden their literacy-related instructional practices. The resource includes lessons and ideas for enhancing existing teaching practices (such as during the whole group read aloud and circle time), and for extending the quality of students' literacy experiences in times that are not typically considered "instructional" (such as during independent reading and play). Ample research evidence shows that when teachers accomplish the types of teaching described in this resource, children's achievement soars—and their lives as literate individuals flourish.

The material in **Literate Days** is organized into three books, each including nine to twelve lessons and reproducibles:

- **BOOK 1:** Grounding Children in Routines and Procedures for Meaningful Learning

- **BOOK 2:** Building, Energizing, and Re-envisioning the Literacy Curriculum

- **BOOK 3:** Deepening the Scholarship in the Classroom Community

- **The DVD:** Lessons from Literate Days

Book 1

The **lessons** in Book 1, implemented within the first weeks of the P/K/1 school year, provide children with the foundation and background they need to successfully pursue a literate life in your classroom. Children learn, through immersion and guided participation in these lessons, the routines and expectations for the different kinds of literacy instruction they will experience in the classroom. For example, they learn what is expected from them at circle time; they try out shared reading, whole-class read-alouds, and a writing workshop; and they are walked through techniques for making smart use of the core centers in your classroom.

Book 1

Grounding Children in
Routines and Procedures
for Meaningful Learning

GRETCHEN OWOCKI

The lessons in *Literate Days* Book 1 provide children with the foundation and background they need to successfully pursue a literate life in your classroom. Children learn, through immersion and guided participation in these lessons, the routines and expectations for the different kinds of literacy instruction they will experience in the classroom.

12 RESEARCH-BASED LESSONS

32 TEACHING TOOLS

13 KIDWATCHING FORMS

The **kidwatching tools** in Book 1 are designed to help you get to know your students and to help you make beginning decisions about how to teach them best. These tools should be used selectively, as they meet your particular students' needs, within your particular curriculum.

Book 2

The **lessons** in Book 2 are designed to offer P/K/1 children continued support as they participate in classroom literacy practices in ever-expanding ways, and are taught new strategies and skills. With the lessons in Book 2, children begin to explore reading and writing strategies in more depth and through more genres; they are introduced to partner reading and independent reading; and they expand their uses of literacy in the centers.

The **kidwatching tools** in Book 2 are designed to help you fine tune what you know about your students, to continue to track their growth over time, and to continue to make instructional decisions based on what they know and can do. These tools should be used selectively, as they meet your particular students' needs, within your particular curriculum.

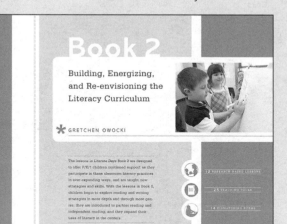

Book 2

Building, Energizing,
and Re-envisioning the
Literacy Curriculum

GRETCHEN OWOCKI

The lessons in *Literate Days* Book 2 are designed to offer P/K/1 children continued support as they participate in these classroom literacy practices in ever-expanding ways, and are taught new strategies and skills. With the lessons in Book 2, children begin to explore reading and writing strategies in more depth and through more genres; they are introduced to partner reading and independent reading; and they expand their uses of literacy in the centers.

12 RESEARCH-BASED LESSONS

25 TEACHING TOOLS

14 KIDWATCHING FORMS

Book 3

The final set of **lessons** takes children deeply into life as literate individuals. Because a child working through this set of lessons requires an understanding of the basic concepts and processes necessary for reading and writing (built through the preschool and kindergarten years), as well as a certain level of independence, it is recommended that these lessons be reserved primarily for late kindergarten and first grade. Kindergarten teachers should choose selectively from Book 3, based on their students' progress with Books 1 and 2. Through Book 3 lessons, children live, experience, and develop

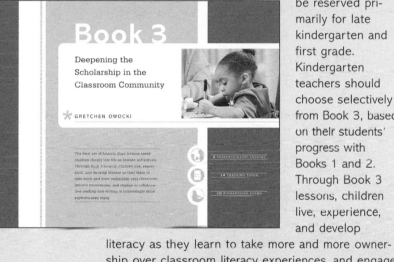

literacy as they learn to take more and more ownership over classroom literacy experiences, and engage in collaborative reading and writing in increasingly more sophisticated ways.

The **kidwatching tools** in Book 3, to be used selectively, are designed to help children become more and more aware of their developing competencies, to learn to self-evaluate, and to continue to inform your instructional practices.

The DVD

Lessons from Literate Days contains 2 hours of classroom footage to help you envision the routines and procedures described in the 33 lessons. You will see preschool, kindergarten, and first grade teachers implementing the lessons, working with children as they participate in related activities, and kidwatching in ways that inform instruction. Brief

follow-up interviews with each teacher are also included. The easy-to-use series of menus on the DVD allows to you navigate quickly to the desired section.

The Lessons

Each lesson begins with a research-supported rationale for its implementation and then offers:

- Detailed plans that include **preparation** information as well as an **introduction,** a **modeling** component, a **scaffolding** component, and a **closure.**

- Teacher resources to be used for the lesson. The teacher resources include planning tools, book lists, and idea lists.

- Child resources to be used for the lesson. The child resources are in the form of talking points, graphic organizers, and classroom visuals. All reproducible forms are offered at the back of each book. You will want to make a copy of (and perhaps even enlarge) many of them to hang nearby as you are teaching.

- Kidwatching and assessment tools related to the concepts taught in the lesson. All reproducible forms are offered at the back of each book. You will want to make a copy of many of them to hang nearby as you are teaching.

Consider the Research

- -

Research findings from well-known scholars is provided as background for each lesson.

BOOK **1** | LESSON 6

Energizing the Writing Center

CONSIDER THE RESEARCH: Children learn to write by writing (NCTE 2004). Through the act of writing, especially in a social setting, they simultaneously develop many understandings, including: how to form letters, spell words, put spaces between words, use punctuation, form a meaningful message, engage an audience, and use the features of a particular genre (Goodman and Wilde 1992; Graves 1982; 1983; Sulzby 1985). To keep children's learning meaningful, make an effort to support them in exploring these competencies simultaneously. Even preschool students should be encouraged to write varied types of meaningful messages, using the understandings and resources they currently have. Sometimes this means that a random string of letters is a "story" or a squiggly line is a "sign." Support even the youngest children in getting ideas on paper, and you are supporting many critical aspects of their literacy development.

Along with creating general workshop time for writing (Lesson 4), set up an inviting writing table for use during center time. For both experiences, children will need to know how to use the materials. This lesson serves that function. After teaching this lesson, allow the students several weeks for open exploration in the center before moving to Book 2 Lesson 8 (Supporting Genre Exploration Through the Writing Center).

33

Lesson Overview

- -

The primary teaching point is presented on each opening page.

**Materials needed for the lesson
are listed as well as suggestions
for classroom arrangement and
differentiation of instruction.**

**Authentic pieces of children's
art produced during Literate Days
lessons are shown.**

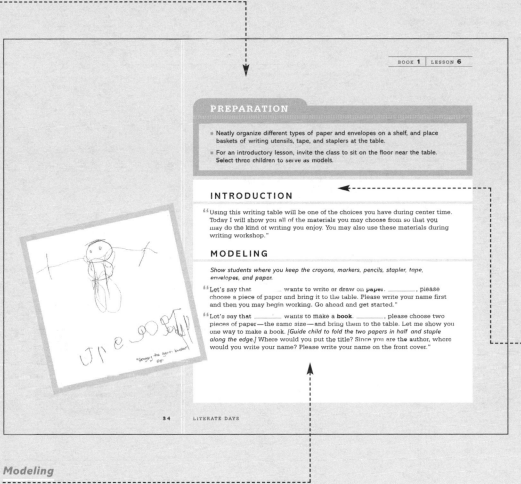

PREPARATION

- Neatly organize different types of paper and envelopes on a shelf, and place baskets of writing utensils, tape, and staplers at the table.
- For an introductory lesson, invite the class to sit on the floor near the table. Select three children to serve as models.

INTRODUCTION

"Using this writing table will be one of the choices you have during center time. Today I will show you all of the materials you may choose from so that you may do the kind of writing you enjoy. You may also use these materials during writing workshop."

MODELING

Show students where you keep the crayons, markers, pencils, stapler, tape, envelopes, and paper.

"Let's say that _____ wants to write or draw on paper. _____, please choose a piece of paper and bring it to the table. Please write your name first and then you may begin working. Go ahead and get started."

"Let's say that _____ wants to make a **book**. _____, please choose two pieces of paper—the same size—and bring them to the table. Let me show you one way to make a book. *[Guide child to fold the two papers in half and staple along the edge.]* Where would you put the title? Since you are the author, where would you write your name? Please write your name on the front cover."

34   LITERATE DAYS

**The language for
introducing the lesson is
modeled and 'stage direc-
tions' for organizing the
classroom, materials, and
children are offered.**

**Teaching language for modeling how
to achieve the lesson goal is presented.**

The Lessons cont.

Scaffolding

Teaching language for supporting the children as they play, work, and learn is presented.

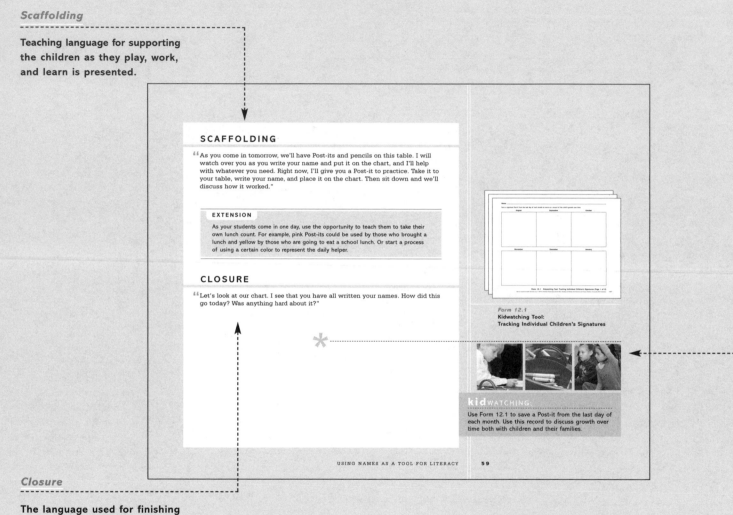

SCAFFOLDING

"As you come in tomorrow, we'll have Post-its and pencils on this table. I will watch over you as you write your name and put it on the chart, and I'll help with whatever you need. Right now, I'll give you a Post-it to practice. Take it to your table, write your name, and place it on the chart. Then sit down and we'll discuss how it worked."

EXTENSION

As your students come in one day, use the opportunity to teach them to take their own lunch count. For example, pink Post-its could be used by those who brought a lunch and yellow by those who are going to eat a school lunch. Or start a process of using a certain color to represent the daily helper.

CLOSURE

"Let's look at our chart. I see that you have all written your names. How did this go today? Was anything hard about it?"

Form 12.1
Kidwatching Tool:
Tracking Individual Children's Signatures

kidWATCHING:
Use Form 12.1 to save a Post-it from the last day of each month. Use this record to discuss growth over time both with children and their families.

USING NAMES AS A TOOL FOR LITERACY   **59**

Kidwatching

Suggestions are made for how to watch children as they play and learn, and special recordkeeping forms are provided.

Closure

The language used for finishing up a lesson is modeled.

Extension

Options for additional work on the lesson goal are introduced.

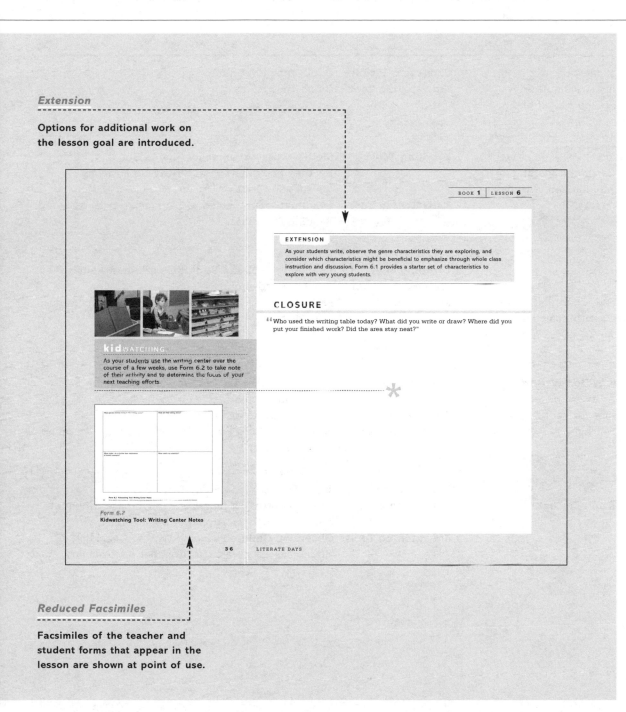

Form 6.2
Kidwatching Tool: Writing Center Notes

BOOK **1** | LESSON **6**

EXTENSION

As your students write, observe the genre characteristics they are exploring, and consider which characteristics might be beneficial to emphasize through whole class instruction and discussion. Form 6.1 provides a starter set of characteristics to explore with very young students.

CLOSURE

"Who used the writing table today? What did you write or draw? Where did you put your finished work? Did the area stay neat?"

kidWATCHING

As your students use the writing center over the course of a few weeks, use Form 6.2 to take note of their activity and to determine the focus of your next teaching efforts.

36 LITERATE DAYS

Reduced Facsimiles

Facsimiles of the teacher and student forms that appear in the lesson are shown at point of use.

The Materials

A preparation list is provided at the beginning of each lesson that outlines the needed materials. Most are commonplace in classrooms. If you want to see in advance the range of materials needed for the entire *Literate Days* program, it is provided here.

- Large Calendar
- Books for shared reading and read-alouds
- Easel and markers
- Pointer
- Post-its
- Wicki Stix (or any wax-covered yarn)
- Highlighting tape
- Name cards
- Red and green file folders
- Paper and pencils
- Alphabet books
- Magnetic letters
- Paper letter tiles
- Blank note cards
- Play-Doh
- Sand
- Paint
- Tape recorder/player
- Earphones

The lessons in each book are listed and briefly described in Figure 1, with core lessons highlighted in gray. While many lessons are taught only one time, or a few times (as follow-ups are needed), core lessons are taught repeatedly throughout the year with variations that allow for introducing different skills or strategies.

Figure 1: **Outline for the 12 *Literate Days* Lessons in Book 1: Grounding Children in Routines and Procedures for Meaningful Learning**

Lesson	Title & Description	Tools & Visuals	
1	**The Morning Circle Routines: Focusing on What Matters** Discuss the routines and expectations for the daily circle gathering: song, greeting, calendar review, shared reading, teacher read-aloud.	Classroom Visual: Kidwatching Tool:	Circle Time Routine Circle Time Notes
2	**Shared Reading: An Assessment-Based Approach** Teach the specific procedures and patterns for the shared reading portion of circle-time—after children have been familiarized with basic circle routines (Lesson 1).	Teaching Tools: Kidwatching Tool:	Mother Goose Rhymes for Shared Reading, Shared Reading Book List, Shared Reading Focus for Instruction Chart Reading Competencies to Emphasize During Shared Reading Checklist
3	**Read-Aloud: Procedures and Early Comprehension Strategy Instruction** Teach specific procedures and patterns for the read-aloud portion of circle-time—after children have been familiarized with basic circle routines (Lesson 1).	Teaching Tool: Classroom Visual: Kidwatching Tool:	Beginning Thinking Strategies for Read-Alouds Teacher Read-Aloud Participation and Engagement in Circle Experiences Checklist
4	**Writing Workshop: Building a Foundation from Which Writers Can Grow** Introduce students to the routines and expectations for your writing workshop.	Teaching Tool: Student Tools: Kidwatching Tool:	Beginning Ideas for Drawing and Writing in a Workshop Setting List Lined paper templates Forms Participation and Engagement in Writing Workshop Checklist Form
5	**Re-envisioning the Alphabet Curriculum** These lessons are designed to support children's early recognition and use of the letters of the alphabet.	Teaching Tool: Student Tools: Kidwatching Tools:	Things to do with Letters List Alphabet Strip, Uppercase & Lowercase Alphabet Assessment Form, Alphabet Book Form Observing Children's Name Writing Checklist, Uppercase & Lowercase Alphabet Assessment Checklist

Gray highlighting indicates core lessons.

continued

Lesson	Title & Description	Tools & Visuals	
6	**Energizing the Writing Center** Introduce and show children how to use and take care of classroom writing materials; discuss how different materials may be used for writing in different genres.	**Teaching Tool:** **Kidwatching Tool:**	Emphasizing Genre Characteristics Talking Points Writing Center Notes
7	**Re-imagining the Library Center** Introduce the organization of the books in the classroom library; discuss expectations for how children will use and handle the materials.	**Classroom Visuals:** **Kidwatching Tools:**	Library Labels, Classroom Library Talking Points Classroom Library Notes, Book Preferences Notes
8	**Taking Full Advantage of the Listening Center** Introduce the listening center and teach different ways of using it throughout the year.	**Teaching Tool:** **Classroom Visuals:** **Student Tools:** **Kidwatching Tool:**	Listening Experiences Listening and Retelling Guide for Fiction, Listening and Retelling Guide for Nonfiction Listening to and Rethinking Fiction, Listening to and Rethinking Nonfiction Listening Center Notes
9	**Building Reading and Writing Skill at the Easel Center** Introduce the easel center and get children started with ideas they might try there.	**Kidwatching Tool:**	Easel Center Notes
10	**Using the Play Center to Facilitate Literacy** Introduce literacy materials to the sociodramatic play area in the classroom, and work with children to enhance their literacy exploration in this area.	**Kidwatching Tool:**	Play Themes Planning Tool
11	**Interactive Writing: Focus on Spelling** Support children in using invented spelling as a resource for writing.	**Teaching Tool:** **Kidwatching Tool:**	Strategies for Writing Ideas List Considering Developmental Phases of Spelling Checklist
12	**Using Names as a Tool for Literacy** This lesson involves children in a study of their own and others' names—as a route to developing many insights into written language.	**Kidwatching Tool:**	Tracking Individual Children's Signatures Forms

Gray highlighting indicates core lessons.

Figure 1: Outline for the 12 *Literate Days* Lessons in Book 2: Building, Energizing, and Re-envisioning the Literacy Curriculum

Lesson	Title & Description	Tools & Visuals	
1	**Expanding the Read-Aloud: Building Strong Comprehenders from the Start** Expand the teacher read-aloud to include an in-depth exploration of comprehension strategies.	Teaching Tool: Classroom Visual:	Teaching Comprehension Strategies Book List, Text for Modeling and Scaffolding *Questioning:* The Enormous Turnip, Text for Modeling and Scaffolding *Visualizing:* Who has seen the wind?, Text for Modeling and Scaffolding *Rethinking:* Red Leaf, Yellow Leaf Overview of Strategies
2	**Using Literature Response as a Tool for Supporting the Development of Content and Literacy Knowledge** Discuss different ways of responding to the content of a book. Make an ongoing list so that students can be independent in choosing response types.	Teaching Tool: Kidwatching Tools:	Responding to Literature Idea List Group Evaluation of Comprehension Strategies Checklist, Individual Evaluation of Comprehension Strategies
3	**Building High-Quality Partner Reading** Walk through the routine and the expectations for partner reading.	Classroom Visuals: Kidwatching Tool:	Partner Reading: Preschool and Early Kindergarten, Partner Reading: Late Kindergarten and First Grade Partner Reading Notes (Whole Class Observations)
4	**Building High-Quality Independent Reading** Walk through the routine and the expectations for independent reading.	Classroom Visual: Kidwatching Tools:	Independent Reading Independent Reading Notes, Tracking Book Handling and Print Concepts Over Time Conference Form
5	**Expanding Use of the Classroom Library: Teaching Children Strategies for Finding Books They Want to Dig Into** Teach children strategies for finding classroom library books they enjoy.	Teaching Tool: Kidwatching Tool:	My Book Preferences Chart Possible Reading Topics Interest Inventory
6	**Previewing as a Channel Into Books** Teach children strategies for previewing text features, illustrations, and words.	Classroom Visual:	Previewing a Book Talking Point

Gray highlighting indicates core lessons.

continued

Lesson	Title & Description	Tools & Visuals	
7	**Expanding the Writing Workshop: Personal and Biographical Narratives** After spending two or three weeks introducing children to the routines and expectations for writing workshop (Book 1 Lesson 6), begin to focus on teaching them to write within particular genres.	**Teaching Tools:** **Student Tool:** **Kidwatching Tool:**	Writing Possibilities Idea List, Narratives and Memoirs About Kids and Family Members Book List Topic Ideas for Writing Planning Form Writing Within the Workshop Setting Checklist
8	**Supporting Genre Exploration Through the Writing Center** Support students in expanding their exploration of genres.	**Teaching Tool:**	Expanding Emphasis on Genre Characteristics Talking Points
9	**Word Study: Focusing on the Essentials** Discuss the different print resources in the classroom that children can use for spelling; study words and word patterns.	**Teaching Tools:** **Student Tools:** **Kidwatching Tool:**	Examples of Print to use as a Spelling Resource Talking Points, Suggested Word List for Preschool, Dolch High Frequency Word Lists, Onset Lists, 37 Most Common Rimes Personal Word List for Spellers, Word and Picture Sorts, Word Challenge Minilessons for Using Spelling Strategies: Kindergarten and First Grade
10	**Expanding Literacy Explorations in Play** Support children in expanding their uses of literacy in the sociodramatic play area.	**Teaching Tool:** **Classroom Visual:** **Kidwatching Tool:**	Play Themes and Literacy Materials Idea List Play Centers Thinking Tool Observing Literacy in Play
11	**Using Print to Support Classroom Activities: Adding to the Genres** Teach children to use print to support various classroom activities.	**Classroom Visual:** **Kidwatching Tool:**	Instruction Form Written Instruction Notes
12	**Using the Classroom Library Checkout System** Teach children to check out books from the classroom library; discuss what they might do with the books at home.	**Teaching Tools:** **Kidwatching Tool:**	Classroom Library Book Check-Out Sheet, Bookmark for Home Reading Reading at Home Notes

Gray highlighting indicates core lessons.

Lesson	Title & Description	Tools & Visuals	
1	**Literature Circles: A Way to Deepen Understanding** Teach the general procedures involved in participating in literature circles and teach children to engage in different collaborative response activities over the course of the school year.	Teaching Tool: Kidwatching Tool:	Collaborative Response Experiences for Literature Circles Idea List Literature Circles Notes
2	**Retelling and Rethinking Stories: A Way to Enhance Experience with Text** Teach children strategies for retelling a story.	Teaching Tool: Classroom Visual: Student Tools: Kidwatching Tool:	Stories for Retelling What to Include in a Retelling: Fiction Retelling Fiction: Problem and Solution Graphic Organizer, Retelling Fiction: Beginning, Middle, End Graphic Organizer Evaluating Story Retelling Over Time
3	**Retelling and Rethinking Nonfiction: A Way to Support Consideration of Key Content** Teach children strategies for retelling nonfiction text.	Classroom Visual: Student Tool: Kidwatching Tool:	What to Include in a Retelling: Nonfiction Retelling Nonfiction Graphic Organizer Evaluating a Nonfiction Retelling
4	**Children Choosing "Just Right" Books to Read** Teach children to choose appropriate texts for various kinds of reading.	Classroom Visual: Kidwatching Tools:	Is This Book Just Right? Evaluating Children's Book Choices Checklist, Self-Evaluation of Recreational Book Reading
5	**Children Evaluating Their Reading: Bringing Learning Activity to a Conscious Level** Teach children to self-evaluate their reading actions and behaviors.	Kidwatching Tool:	Self-Evaluation of Reading (Teacher's Record)
6	**Writing a Story: Elevating the Workshop Experience** After children gain experience with writing in a workshop setting (Book 1 Lesson 6), and writing personal and biographical narratives (Book 2 Lesson 7), extend your instruction into new genres. The present lesson is designed to teach students a way to craft a story that involves a problem-resolution sequence.	Teaching Tool: Classroom Visual: Student Tools:	Possible Minilessons for Piper's Story Child's Story to Use for Instruction Planning to Write a Story Graphic Organizer

Gray highlighting indicates core lessons.

continued

Lesson	Title & Description	Tools & Visuals	
7	**Writing Nonfiction (Focus on Description): Elevating the Workshop Experience** After children gain experience with writing in a workshop setting (Book 1 Lesson 6), and writing personal and biographical narratives (Book 2 Lesson 7), extend your instruction into new genres. The present lesson is designed to teach students a way to craft a non-fiction piece using the "description" text structure.	**Teaching Tool:** **Classroom Visual:** **Student Tools:**	Possible Minilessons Using Preston's Description Child's Description to Use for Instruction Planning to Write a Description: Notes, Planning to Write a Descriptive Piece Graphic Organizer
8	**Writing (and Reading) Poetry (Focus on Free Verse): Elevating the Workshop Experience** Teach students to listen to the voices of poets, and get them started writing their own poetry.	**Teaching Tool:** **Classroom Visual:**	Questions for Thinking about Poetry Haiku Examples
9	**Children Evaluating Their Writing: Bringing Learning Activity to a Conscious Level** Teach children to self-evaluate various components of their writing.	**Kidwatching Tool:**	Self-Evaluation of Writing Form

Gray highlighting indicates core lessons.

Students will benefit from experiencing the curriculum for more than one year. The concepts taught in each lesson are fundamental to literacy, and should be explored regularly throughout the early childhood years. Regardless of grade level (preschool, kindergarten, or first grade), you should start with Book 1 and then move on to Book 2, with younger students being given more time to move through the books than older students. Book 3 is designed primarily for first-grade students, but depending on the class and the students, kindergarten teachers may wish to move into parts or this entire book as well. It is suggested that first-grade teachers move into Book 3 around November or December (repeating core lessons from Books 1 and 2 throughout the year). Kindergarten teachers may move into Book 3 (if their students have progressed that far) around January or February.

Some lessons (referred to as **core** lessons) are implemented many times — with variations to emphasize multiple skills and strategies — throughout the year. For example, the shared reading lesson is used to teach many different reading skills and strategies, and is therefore implemented regularly (daily), throughout the year, in each grade.

In terms of what order to teach the lessons in, the nine to twelve lessons in each book could be taught in the order in which they are packaged. However, you will want to review the entire set to determine whether presentation in a different order might suit your students better.

Figure 2 lays out a possible yearly implementation plan for the three grades. Figures 3, 4, and 5 lay out examples of pathways for the implementation of each lesson by grade. However, these should be used just to get a general idea of what a schedule might look like. We've provided a blank schedule (Figure 5) for you to write out your own. You will find the most success by planning for a month or so at a time, and implementing the lessons as it seems appropriate.

Plan for the Year	Preschool	Kindergarten	First Grade
BOOK 1	September–October	September	September
BOOK 2	November–June *Continue with core* Book 1 lessons as Book 2 lessons are introduced.*	October–January	October–November
BOOK 3		January–June *Select Book 3 lessons as individual students or groups of students indicate readiness, continuing with core Book 1 and 2 lessons.*	November–June *Continue with core Book 1 and 2 lessons as Book 3 lessons are introduced.*

*Core lessons are implemented many times.

Figure 3: **Example of a Pathway for Preschool**

Book-Lesson	Focus	1	2	3	4	5	6	7	8	9	10	11	12	13	14	15	16	17	18	19	20	21	22	23	24	25	26	27	28	29	30	31	32	33	34	35	36
1-1	Circle Routines and Expectations	✓																																			
1-2	Shared Reading/Print Processing			✓	✓	✓	✓	✓	✓	✓	✓	✓	✓	✓	✓	✓	✓	✓	✓	✓	✓	✓	✓	✓	✓	✓	✓	✓	✓	✓	✓	✓	✓	✓	✓	✓	✓
1-3	Read-Aloud/Comprehension			✓	✓	✓	✓	✓	✓	✓	✓	✓	✓	✓	✓	✓	✓	✓	✓	Switch to lesson 2-1. →→→→→→→→→→→→→→→→→→																	
1-4	Writing Workshop: Early Phases	✓	✓	✓	✓	✓	✓	✓	✓	✓	✓	✓	✓	✓	✓	✓	✓	✓	✓	✓	✓	✓	Switch to lesson 2-7. →→→→→→→→→→→→→→														
1-5	Alphabet		✓	✓	✓	✓	✓	✓	✓	✓	✓	✓	✓	✓	✓	✓	✓	✓	✓	✓	✓	✓	✓	✓	✓	✓	✓	✓	✓	✓	✓	✓	✓	✓	✓	✓	✓
1-6	Writing Center	✓		Switch to lesson 2-8. →→																																	
1-7	Library Center		✓																																		
1-8	Listening Center	✓					✓							✓							✓						✓						✓				
1-9	Easel Center			✓																																	
1-10	Play Center			✓	✓	✓	✓	✓	✓	✓	Switch to lesson 2-10. →→→→→→→→→→→→→→→→→→→→→→→→→→→→→→→→→→																										
1-11	Interactive Writing/Writing Skill				✓	✓	✓	✓	✓	✓	✓	✓	✓	✓	✓	✓	✓	✓	✓	✓	✓	✓	✓	✓	✓	✓	✓	✓	✓	✓	✓	✓	✓	✓	✓	✓	✓
1-12	Names: Reading and Writing		✓																																		
2-1	Read-Aloud/Comprehension	Lesson 1-3 first. →→→→→→→→→→→→→→→→→→→→→→→→→→→																		✓	✓	✓	✓	✓	✓	✓	✓	✓	✓	✓	✓	✓	✓	✓	✓	✓	✓
2-2	Literature Response	Lesson 1-3 first and 2-1 first. →→→→→→→→→→→→→→→→→→→→→→→→																				✓	✓	✓	✓	✓	✓	✓	✓	✓	✓	✓	✓	✓	✓	✓	✓
2-3	Partner Reading													✓																							
2-4	Independent Reading												✓																								
2-5	Choosing Books	Lesson 1-6 first. →→→→→→→→→→→→→→→→→→→→→→→												✓										✓													
2-6	Previewing Books											✓				✓					✓						✓							✓			
2-7	Writing Workshop: Narratives	Lesson 1-4 first. →→→→→→→→→→→→→→→→→→→→→→→→→→→→→→→→																					✓	✓	✓	✓	✓	✓	✓	✓	✓	✓	✓	✓	✓	✓	✓
2-8	Writing Center	Lesson 1-5 first. →→→→→→→→→→→→→→→→										✓		✓		✓			✓			✓		✓			✓			✓			✓				
2-9	Phonics and Word Study										✓	✓	✓	✓	✓	✓	✓	✓	✓	✓	✓	✓	✓	✓	✓	✓	✓	✓	✓	✓	✓	✓	✓	✓	✓	✓	✓
2-10	Play Center	Lesson 1-9 first. →→→→→→→→→→→→→→→→										✓			✓			✓			✓			✓			✓			✓			✓				
2-11	Using Written Instructions																	✓				✓			✓			✓			✓			✓			
2-12	Checking Out a Book									✓																											
3-1	Literature Circles																																				
3-2	Literature Response: Fiction																																				
3-3	Literature Response: Nonfiction																																				
3-4	Choosing Books																																				
3-5	Self-Evaluation of Reading																																				
3-6	Writing Workshop: Fiction																																				
3-7	Writing Workshop: Nonfiction																																				
3-8	Writing Workshop: Poetry																																				
3-9	Self-Evaluation of Writing																																				

Week		1	2	3	4	5	6	7	8	9	10	11	12	13	14	15	16	17	18	19	20	21	22	23	24	25	26	27	28	29	30	31	32	33	34	35	36
Book-Lesson	**Focus**																																				
1-1	Circle Routines and Expectations	✓																																			
1-2	Shared Reading/Print Processing		✓	✓	✓	✓	✓	✓	✓	✓	✓	✓	✓	✓	✓	✓	✓	✓	✓	✓	✓	✓	✓	✓	✓	✓	✓	✓	✓	✓	✓	✓	✓	✓	✓	✓	✓
1-3	Read-Aloud/Comprehension		✓	✓	✓	✓	✓	✓	✓	✓	✓	Switch to lesson 2-1. →																									
1-4	Writing Workshop: Early Phases	✓	✓	✓	✓	✓	✓	Switch to lesson 2-7. →																													
1-5	Alphabet		✓	✓	✓	✓	✓	✓	✓	✓	✓	✓	✓	✓	✓	✓	✓	✓	✓	Assess and switch to small groups, based on need. →																	
1-6	Writing Center	✓	✓	✓	✓	✓	✓	Switch to lesson 2-8. →																													
1-7	Library Center			✓																																	
1-8	Listening Center	✓					✓							✓							✓						✓							✓			
1-9	Easel Center			✓																																	
1-10	Play Center		✓	✓	✓	✓	✓	✓	✓	Switch to lesson 2-10. →																											
1-11	Interactive Writing/Writing Skill			✓	✓	✓	✓	✓	✓	✓	✓	✓	✓	✓	✓	✓	✓	✓	✓	✓	✓	✓	✓	✓	✓	✓	✓	✓	✓	✓	✓	✓	✓	✓	✓	✓	✓
1-12	Names: Reading and Writing			✓																																	
2-1	Read-Aloud/Comprehension	Lesson 1-3 first. →										✓	✓	✓	✓	✓	✓	✓	✓	✓	✓	✓	✓	✓	✓	✓	✓	✓	✓	✓	✓	✓	✓	✓	✓	✓	✓
2-2	Literature Response	Lesson 1-3 first. →											✓	✓	✓	✓	✓	✓	✓	✓	✓	✓	✓	✓	✓	✓	✓	✓	✓	✓	✓	✓	✓	✓	✓	✓	✓
2-3	Partner Reading								✓																												
2-4	Independent Reading							✓																													
2-5	Choosing Books	Lesson 1-6 first. →							✓					✓																							
2-6	Previewing Books								✓					✓							✓						✓							✓			
2-7	Writing Workshop: Narratives	Lesson 1-4 first. →						✓	✓	✓	✓	✓	✓	✓	✓	✓	✓	✓	✓	✓	✓	✓	✓	✓	✓	✓	✓	✓	✓	✓	✓	✓	✓	✓	✓	✓	✓
2-8	Writing Center	Lesson 1-5 first. →						✓		✓		✓		✓		✓		✓		✓		✓		✓		✓		✓		✓		✓		✓		✓	
2-9	Phonics and Word Study			✓	✓	✓	✓	✓	✓	✓	✓	✓	✓	✓	✓	✓	✓	✓	✓	✓	✓	✓	✓	✓	✓	✓	✓	✓	✓	✓	✓	✓	✓	✓	✓	✓	✓
2-10	Play Center	Lesson 1-9 first. →								✓			✓			✓			✓			✓			✓			✓			✓			✓			
2-11	Using Written Instructions				✓			✓			✓			✓			✓			✓			✓			✓			✓			✓			✓		
2-12	Checking Out a Book					✓																															
3-1	Literature Circles	Lessons 1-3 and 2-2 first. →																	✓	✓	✓	✓	✓	✓	✓	✓	✓	✓	✓	✓	✓	✓	✓	✓	✓	✓	✓
3-2	Literature Response: Fiction	Lessons 1-3 and 2-1 first. →																	Offer periodic opportunities for retelling. →																		
3-3	Literature Response: Nonfiction	Lessons 1-3 and 2-1 first. →																	Offer periodic opportunities for retelling. →																		
3-4	Choosing Books																			✓ Teach as needed →																	
3-5	Self-Evaluation of Reading																			✓			✓			✓			✓			✓			✓		
3-6	Writing Workshop: Fiction	Lessons 1-4, 2-7, and 3-2 first. →																	✓	✓	✓	✓							✓	✓	✓	✓					
3-7	Writing Workshop: Nonfiction	Lessons 1-4 and 2-7 first. →																		✓	✓	✓	✓	✓													
3-8	Writing Workshop: Poetry																																	✓	✓	✓	✓
3-9	Self-Evaluation of Writing														✓			✓			✓			✓			✓			✓			✓				

Figure 5: Example of a Pathway for First Grade

Book-Lesson	Focus	1	2	3	4	5	6	7	8	9	10	11	12	13	14	15	16	17	18	19	20	21	22	23	24	25	26	27	28	29	30	31	32	33	34	35	36
1-1	Circle Routines and Expectations	✓																																			
1-2	Shared Reading/Print Processing		✓	✓	✓	✓	✓	✓	✓	✓	✓	✓	✓	✓	✓	✓	✓	✓	✓	✓	✓	✓	✓	✓	✓	✓	✓	✓	✓	✓	✓	✓	✓	✓	✓	✓	✓
1-3	Read-Aloud/Comprehension		✓	✓	✓	Switch to lesson 2-1. →																															
1-4	Writing Workshop: Early Phases	✓	✓	✓	✓	Switch to lesson 2-7. →																															
1-5	Alphabet	Assess and switch to small groups, based on need. →																																			
1-6	Writing Center	✓																																			
1-7	Library Center	✓																																			
1-8	Listening Center	✓					✓				✓				✓				✓				✓				✓				✓				✓		
1-9	Easel Center				✓																																
1-10	Play Center		✓	✓	✓	✓	Switch to lesson 2-10. →																														
1-11	Interactive Writing/Writing Skill	✓	✓	✓	✓	✓	✓	✓	✓	✓	✓	✓	✓	✓	✓	✓	✓	✓	✓	✓	✓	✓	✓	✓	✓	✓	✓	✓	✓	✓	✓	✓	✓	✓	✓	✓	✓
1-12	Names: Reading and Writing		✓																																		
2-1	Read-Aloud/Comprehension	Lesson 1-3 first. ✓	✓	✓	✓	✓	✓	✓	✓	✓	✓	✓	✓	✓	✓	✓	✓	✓	✓	✓	✓	✓	✓	✓	✓	✓	✓	✓	✓	✓	✓	✓	✓	✓	✓	✓
2-2	Literature Response	Lesson 1-3 first. →					✓	✓	✓	✓	✓	✓	✓	✓	✓	✓	✓	✓	✓	✓	✓	✓	✓	✓	✓	✓	✓	✓	✓	✓	✓	✓	✓	✓	✓	✓
2-3	Partner Reading						✓																														
2-4	Independent Reading					✓																															
2-5	Choosing Books	Lesson 1-6 first. →						✓							✓																						
2-6	Phonics and Word Study								✓					✓					✓					✓					✓								
2-7	Writing Workshop: Narratives	Lesson 1-4 first.			✓	✓	✓	✓	✓	Switch to lesson 3-6 and 3-7. →																											
2-8	Writing Center	Lesson 1-5 first. →						✓		✓		✓		✓		✓		✓		✓		✓		✓		✓		✓		✓		✓		✓		✓	
2-9	Phonics and Word Study				✓	✓	✓	✓	✓	✓	✓	✓	✓	✓	✓	✓	✓	✓	✓	✓	✓	✓	✓	✓	✓	✓	✓	✓	✓	✓	✓	✓	✓	✓	✓	✓	✓
2-10	Play Center	Lesson 1-9 first. →						✓		✓		✓		✓		✓		✓		✓		✓		✓		✓		✓		✓		✓		✓			
2-11	Using Written Instructions					✓		✓		✓		✓		✓		✓		✓		✓		✓		✓		✓		✓		✓		✓			✓		
2-12	Checking Out a Book						✓																														
3-1	Literature Circles	Lessons 1-3 and 2-2 first. →								✓	✓	✓	✓	✓	✓	✓	✓	✓	✓	✓	✓	✓	✓	✓	✓	✓	✓	✓	✓	✓	✓	✓	✓	✓	✓	✓
3-2	Literature Response: Fiction	Lessons 1-3 and 2-1 first. →								Offer periodic opportunities for retelling. →																											
3-3	Literature Response: Nonfiction	Lessons 1-3 and 2-1 first. →								Offer periodic opportunities for retelling. →																											
3-4	Choosing Books						✓				✓				✓				✓	Teach as needed. →																	
3-5	Self-Evaluation of Reading									✓			✓			✓			✓			✓			✓			✓			✓			✓			
3-6	Writing Workshop: Fiction									✓	✓	✓	✓							✓	✓	✓	✓										Student Choice →				
3-7	Writing Workshop: Nonfiction														✓	✓	✓	✓							✓	✓	✓	✓	✓	✓			Student Choice →				
3-8	Writing Workshop: Poetry																																Student Choice →				
3-9	Self-Evaluation of Writing						✓				✓			✓			✓			✓			✓			✓			✓			✓					

Figure 6: Blank Form for Planning

Week		1	2	3	4	5	6	7	8	9	10	11	12	13	14	15	16	17	18	19	20	21	22	23	24	25	26	27	28	29	30	31	32	33	34	35	36
Book-Lesson	**Focus**																																				
1-1	Circle Routines and Expectations																																				
1-2	Shared Reading/Print Processing																																				
1-3	Read-Aloud/Comprehension																																				
1-4	Writing Workshop: Early Phases																																				
1-5	Alphabet																																				
1-6	Writing Center																																				
1-7	Library Center																																				
1-8	Listening Center																																				
1-9	Easel Center																																				
1-10	Play Center																																				
1-11	Interactive Writing/Writing Skill																																				
1-12	Names: Reading and Writing																																				
2-1	Read-Aloud/Comprehension																																				
2-2	Literature Response																																				
2-3	Partner Reading																																				
2-4	Independent Reading																																				
2-5	Choosing Books																																				
2-6	Previewing Books																																				
2-7	Writing Workshop: Narratives																																				
2-8	Writing Center																																				
2-9	Phonics and Word Study																																				
2-10	Play Center																																				
2-11	Using Written Instructions																																				
2-12	Checking Out a Book																																				
3-1	Literature Circles																																				
3-2	Literature Response: Fiction																																				
3-3	Literature Response: Nonfiction																																				
3-4	Choosing Books																																				
3-5	Self-Evaluation of Reading																																				
3-6	Writing Workshop: Fiction																																				
3-7	Writing Workshop: Nonfiction																																				
3-8	Writing Workshop: Poetry																																				
3-9	Self-Evaluation of Writing																																				

Literate Days:
Tailoring for Individual Needs and Grade Level

Three key resources will aid in teaching the lessons in ways that are responsive to individual needs and to different grade levels:

■ First, most lessons include kidwatching tools that help identify students' particular strengths and needs. A key to developmental instruction is to understand where students are in their development, and to then teach toward their likely next steps.

■ Second, various tips for adapting lessons for more and less skilled/experienced readers and writers are provided throughout the lessons and as part of some kidwatching tools.

■ Third, a developmental continuum (Figure 7) gives an overview of the developmental capabilities typically exhibited by students in each of the grades. You will want to benchmark children's progress on the continuum and use the information to guide their next steps in instruction. The continuum should not be used as a guide for testing, but rather as an informal tool to guide observation, reflection, and planning. Consider preparing a form for each student and using it to identify and track developing competencies.

Continuum of Competencies	Many preschoolers	Many kindergartners	Many first graders
Participation in Classroom Literacy Practices	■ with consistent guidance related to routines and procedures, actively participate in classroom literacy practices	■ with intermittent guidance related to routines and procedures, self-monitor and stay focused while participating in classroom literacy practices	■ self-monitor and stay focused while participating in classroom literacy practices
	■ express ideas about literacy as they work and play with peers	■ respond to text and listen to peers' responses; exchange ideas about writing	■ engage in reading and writing discussions that serve to enhance content knowledge and literacy knowledge
Attitude and Interest	■ express enthusiasm about fiction, nonfiction, and poetry	■ express enthusiasm about fiction, nonfiction, and poetry	■ express enthusiasm about fiction, nonfiction, and poetry
	■ name some favorite books	■ name some favorite books and authors	■ name several books and authors, articulating reasons for particular tastes and preferences
	■ locate favorite books within the classroom library	■ locate favorite books within the classroom library; critique and articulate reasons for preferences	■ locate favorite books within the classroom library, critique and describe their value, and make recommendations to peers
	■ choose topics of interest for drawing and writing	■ choose topics of interest and personal significance for drawing and writing, describing some specific topic preferences for writing	■ choose topics of interest and personal significance for writing, describing topic and genre preferences

continued

Continuum of Competencies	Many preschoolers	Many kindergartners	Many first graders
Text Comprehension Knowledge and Strategies	■ demonstrate understanding of vocabulary occurring frequently in preschool level texts	■ demonstrate understanding of vocabulary occurring frequently in texts used in kindergarten	■ demonstrate understanding of vocabulary occurring frequently in texts used in first grade
	■ with guidance describe real-life experiences that texts bring to mind	■ describe connections to text/prior knowledge about text	■ describe in depth connections to text/prior knowledge about text and ways such connections/knowledge aid meaning making
	■ point out connections between texts	■ talk about connections between texts (with increasing depth over the year)	■ reflect on connections between texts (with increasing depth over the year) and ways they help to build world knowledge
	■ make predictions about text content	■ make predictions about text content and word meanings, reflecting on outcomes of the predictions	■ make predictions about text content and word meanings, explaining rationale and reflecting on outcomes
	■ monitor and discuss meaning (often literal) as it develops over the course of a text	■ monitor meaning and notice breakdowns	■ monitor meaning and take action at breakdowns
	■ ask questions (often literal) and, with guidance, speculate on and search for answers	■ ask questions and speculate on answers/ways to search for answers; find some answers by reviewing illustrations	■ ask questions and speculate on answers/ways to search for answers; find some answers by reading
	■ use drama/ movement to reflect on visual images evoked by a reading	■ describe visual images and emotions evoked by a reading	■ describe visual images and emotions evoked by a reading, and their role in meaning making
	■ discuss text interpretations (often literal) and inferences about characters and events	■ discuss text interpretations (that go beyond the literal) and inferences about characters and events, recognizing when an inference is occurring	■ discuss text interpretations and how and why they differ among readers; discuss inferences about characters and events and discuss role of inferring in reading

continued

Continuum of Competencies	Many preschoolers	Many kindergartners	Many first graders
Text Comprehension Knowledge and Strategies cont.	■ use books as a prop for rethinking and retelling familiar text ■ begin to discuss different text formats and genre characteristics	■ with or without props, retell some of the key events and information gained from fiction and nonfiction ■ discuss text formats and genre characteristics (including character, setting, problem, and resolution in fiction, and descriptive and sequential formats in nonfiction); use knowledge of text format to hypothesize what varied text says (for example, predict food names when looking at a menu) ■ with teacher support, use graphic organizers to organize thinking about text	■ without props, retell fiction including an ordered sequence of major story elements; retell key information gained from nonfiction ■ describe different text formats and genre characteristics; begin to attend to format as a tool for meaning making in reading ■ use graphic organizers to organize thinking about text ■ describe several comprehension strategies and how each fosters meaning
Phonological Awareness	■ orally play with words and rhymes through songs, read-alouds, and games ■ predict rhyming words when listening to rhyming text read aloud	■ identify and supply words with the same onset (bat-big) or the same rime (bat-cat). ■ orally segment words into sounds/chunks; orally blend sounds/chunks into words	■ identify and supply words with the same onset (bat-big) or the same rime (bat-cat). ■ orally segment words into sounds/chunks; orally blend sounds/chunks into words; easily and automatically use these capabilities to support writing and reading
Letter Identification and Formation	■ name some letters, often starting with those in own name ■ write some letters and/or letter-like symbols	■ name all uppercase and lowercase letters (sometimes mixing up letters that look alike) ■ form legible letters (often in uppercase or mixture of upper and lower) ■ with support, form most letters automatically as they are needed in writing	■ easily name all uppercase and lowercase letters ■ form legible upper and lowercase letters ■ form letters automatically, as they are needed in writing

continued

Continuum of Competencies	Many preschoolers	Many kindergartners	Many first graders
Orthographic/ Spelling Knowledge	▪ use letters or letter-like symbols to represent meaning	▪ use letters to represent meaning	
	▪ match a few speech sounds to letters	▪ match many speech sounds to letters	▪ match many speech sounds to letters/letter patterns
	▪ begin to listen for/articulate prominent sounds or chunks while spelling	▪ represent one or two prominent sounds in a word (may not read back own writing)	▪ represent all of the prominent sounds in words
	▪ spell some words conventionally (often starting with own name)	▪ spell several words conventionally (may exhibit less mature spelling when working on complex pieces)	▪ conventionally spell many commonly used words, continuing to invent as necessary
		▪ demonstrate some knowledge of spelling patterns and use that knowledge to generate new spellings	▪ demonstrate knowledge of many spelling patterns and use that knowledge to generate new spellings
	▪ copy some words as an alternative to inventing	▪ with support, use some classroom print resources to support spelling	▪ independently use a variety of print resources to support spelling.
	▪ show some awareness of notion of convention in spelling	▪ show awareness of notion of convention; may become tentative about inventing spellings	▪ show concern for spelling and awareness of words that may be incorrect

continued

Continuum of Competencies	Many preschoolers	Many kindergartners	Many first graders
Book Handling and Text Processing	▪ appropriately orient and turn pages of a book; explore directionality of print	▪ use appropriate directionality when reading or pretending to read print	▪ consistently use appropriate directionality when reading
	▪ understand that pictures are viewed and print is read	▪ understand the functions of different parts of a book	▪ understand the functions of different parts of books and begin to attend to some parts independently
	▪ attend to pictures, often labeling rather than telling a connected sequence of events	▪ use pictures to tell story or connected sequence of events	▪ use pictures smartly, as a cue to support meaning making while decoding
	▪ begin to notice and discuss words and word features (often using incorrect terms)	▪ appropriately use many literacy-related terms, such as "letter" and "word"	▪ appropriately use many literacy-related terms, such as "letter," "word," "table of contents," and "period."
	▪ recognize some familiar words- or hypothesize words based on first letter	▪ automatically recognize some written words	▪ automatically recognize many written words (demonstrating steady progress across the year)
	▪ read holistically (using what is remembered from previous reading in combination with own insights and use of print and picture cues)	▪ track and read simple text (independently or while listening to an adult), especially if it is familiar; read picture books containing a few lines per page	▪ track and read with comprehension and accuracy increasingly more complex text; read short picture books
	▪ ask questions (or lose interest) when text becomes confusing	▪ begin to monitor meaning and begin to self-correct using meaning, structure, and letter cues	▪ monitor meaning and self-correct using meaning, structure, and letter cues
	▪ discuss similarities and differences in the ways words look	▪ use fix-up strategies as appropriate (reread, read on, word analysis)	▪ use fix-up strategies as appropriate (reread, read on, word analysis)
		▪ analyze words (may focus only on beginning or beginning and end of word; may utter letters or sounds without blending)	▪ analyze words (blending by sound or chunk; trying different sounds)
		▪ read aloud with some word-by-word and some fluent phrasing	▪ read aloud with appropriate fluency (which varies depending on text difficulty and content)

continued

Continuum of Competencies	Many preschoolers	Many kindergartners	Many first graders
Writing Knowledge and Processes	▪ experiment with writing in varied genres, such as signs, lists, notes, and labels (often during sociodramatic play)	▪ experiment with writing in varied genres, including personal narratives, fiction, and nonfiction	▪ use written language to serve many authentic purposes; compose personal narratives, fiction, nonfiction, and poetry
	▪ make decisions about what to draw and write	▪ with teacher support, brainstorm ideas for content and structure of written pieces	▪ brainstorm ideas for content and structure of written pieces; use graphic organizers for planning
	▪ demonstrate 1-2 conventional genre characteristics per piece	▪ demonstrate several conventional genre characteristics per piece	▪ conventionally use numerous features specific to each genre
	▪ mix drawing with writing and use of other symbol systems (such as talk, movement, and sound) to convey meaning	▪ write with focus, using drawing to help convey meaning	▪ write with focus, using connected sentences in a logical sequence
	▪ begin to write left to write and top to bottom	▪ use proper directionality, sometimes breaking this pattern	▪ consistently use proper directionality
	▪ talk about written words, sounds, and letters	▪ begin to space words appropriately	▪ appropriately space between words
	▪ play with punctuation marks	▪ explore punctuation	▪ conventionally use some punctuation
	▪ discuss the concept of capital and lowercase letters	▪ explore capitalization	▪ capitalize beginnings of sentences and some proper nouns (not always consistently)
	▪ begin to notice need for simple editing (for example, a missing letter in a name).	▪ make an attempt to write in ways that others will be able to read; begin to make spelling and content edits/revisions based on rereading, reading aloud, and collaborating	▪ create pieces that communicate effectively; make spelling and content edits/revisions based on rereading, reading aloud, and collaborating

Three sources supported the development of this continuum:

1. Burns, Griffin, and Snow (1999). Starting Out Right: A Guide to Promoting Children's Reading Success. National Academy Press.

2. A Position statement of the International Reading Association and the National Association for the Education of Young Children. 1998. Learning to Read and Write: Developmentally Appropriate Practices for Young Children.

3. Michigan Department of Education. Grade Level Content Expectations: English Language Arts Across the Grades. www.michigan.gov/mde

Literate Days:

Setting Up for Literate Days

Exemplary literacy teachers build well-managed classrooms, thus freeing themselves to provide extensive and rich instruction (Taylor, Pearson, Clark, and Walpole 2000; Pressley, Allington, Wharton-McDonald, Block, & Morrow 2001). Managing a classroom well requires working toward predictable but engaging daily routines in which children have the resources they need to work and make decisions without constant direction from the teacher. It requires immersing children in a community of practice, and then providing explicit instruction so that children know how to appropriately and successfully engage in the discourses of that community. And it requires an effort to ensure a sense of warmth and helpfulness in the learning community, so that children may proceed with the knowledge that they are respected, trusted, and cared about.

Figures 8, 9, and 10 provide examples of daily schedules that allow for the teaching of the lessons in this resource. Each schedule includes a circle meeting for shared reading and a read-aloud, a reading workshop for varied kinds of reading and center activities, and a writing workshop.

Figure 11 provides an example of a center schedule for students to follow. The five activities on the top row of the center schedule are core centers — to be introduced early in the year and carried out throughout the year. (The lessons in Book 1 and Book 2 provide suggestions and ideas for developing the centers.) At center time, students work in five groups, each with up to six children. Each group has two center choices (the top row of "cores" and the bottom row of "supplementals.") To indicate to groups when it is time to rotate, the teacher rotates the group of names at the top of the schedule. A teacher wishing to have all of the students use all of the centers in a week would rotate the names every day. A teacher wishing to have all of the students use all of the centers over the course of a month might rotate the names at the beginning of each week. Early on, rather than giving each group of children two choices for center time, you might want to start with just one choice, or five centers that you have taught and the children are comfortable using. Figure 12 offers a set of ideas for differentiating instruction within the centers.

Figure 8: **Planning Tool: Daily Schedule (Example for Preschool Teacher)**

8:25   First Circle Meeting

    8:25   Song, Greeting, Review of Day (Calendar)

            (Any new centers, center activities, or classroom procedures may be introduced at this time.)

    8:30   Shared Reading (Poems, Rhymes, Big Books) with contextualized strategy and skill instruction

    8:35   Read-Aloud (Engaging literature— often related to science or social studies themes)

8:45   Literacy Workshop

    8:45   Literacy/Play Centers Begin (centers are integrated with science, social studies, and math themes.)

            The beginning of center time may be used to introduce new activities. As children work in centers, provide individualized instruction. Occasionally pull together small groups of children for instruction.

9:30   Clean Up/Restroom/Outdoor Play/Snack

10:05   Circle Meeting

    10:05   Movement and Music

    10:15   Minilesson and whole group experience/center experience involving writing, science, social studies or math

10:45   Clean Up

10:55   Read Aloud

11:10   Dismissal

Time guidelines for the circle meeting are approximate. Carefully plan the amount of time to be spent on each activity so that the meeting lasts no longer than about 20 minutes. For example, if a long text is used for Shared Reading, a shorter text is chosen for the Read-Aloud.

Morning Itinerary

8:20 Arrival, Sign In, Informal Conversation

8:25 Circle Meeting

    8:25 Song, Greeting, Review of Day (Calendar)

        (Any new centers, center activities, or classroom procedures may be introduced at this time.)

    8:30 Shared Reading (Poems, Rhymes, Big Books) with contextualized strategy and skill instruction

    8:40 Read-Aloud (Engaging literature — often related to science or social studies themes)

8:50 Reading Workshop

    8:50 Response to the Read-Aloud Literature or Partner Reading

        Optional: This may be used on same days for additional strategy instruction, letter and word study, or to introduce new procedures and activities.

9:00 Literacy Centers Begin (Many centers are integrated with science and social studies themes.) As children work in centers, provide individualized instruction to three small groups (5–15 minutes each) and conference individually with students. The amount of time you spend with groups will depend on the age of your students and your personal preferences as a teacher. The group instruction may be organized for guided reading, word work, phonics concepts, building interest in reading, reading comprehension, and so on.

9:30 Restroom/Outdoor Play/Snack

9:55 Writing Workshop

    9:55 Minilesson Related to Writing or Spelling

10:05 Writing/Individual or Small Group Conferences with Teacher

10:20 Reflections on Writing

10:25 Exploring Our World (Science and Social Studies)

10:45 Math

11:05 Clean Up

11:10 Dismissal

Time guidelines for the circle meeting are approximate. Carefully plan the amount of time to be spent on each activity so that the meeting lasts no longer than about 20 minutes. For example, if a long text is used for Shared Reading, a shorter text is chosen for the Read-Aloud.

Figure 10: **Planning Tool: Daily Schedule (Example for Full-Day Kindergarten or First Grade)**

8:20 Arrival, Sign In, Informal Conversation

8:30 Circle Meeting

    8:30 Song, Greeting, Review of Day (Calendar)

    (Any new centers, center activities, or classroom procedures may be introduced at this time or at 10:00.)

    8:35 Shared Reading (Poems, Rhymes, Big Books) with contextualized strategy and skill instruction

    8:45 Read-Aloud (Engaging literature—often related to science or social studies themes.)

8:55 Reading Workshop

    8:55 Response to the Read-Aloud Literature (Independent or Small Group)

    9:10 Independent or Partner Reading

    9:20 Literacy Centers Begin (Many centers are integrated with science and social studies themes)

10:00 Meeting

This time may be used for additional strategy instruction, reflections and sharing from reading workshop, letter or word study, or to introduce new procedures and activities.

10:20 Outdoor Play/Restroom/Snack

10:40 Writing Workshop

    10:40 Minilesson related to writing or spelling

    10:50 Writing/Individual or Small Group Conferences with Teacher

11:10 Morning Reflections

11:20 Lunch and Outdoor Play/Restroom

Time guidelines for the circle meeting are approximate. Carefully plan the amount of time to be spent on each activity so that the meeting lasts no longer than about 20 minutes. For example, if a long text is used for Shared Reading, a shorter text is chosen for the Read-Aloud.

12:10 Exploring Our World (Science and Social Studies)

1:00 Special (Art, Music, Physical Education)

1:40 Snack/Restroom

1:55 Math

2:30 Afternoon Reflections or Read-Aloud

2:35 Clean Up

3:00 Dismissal

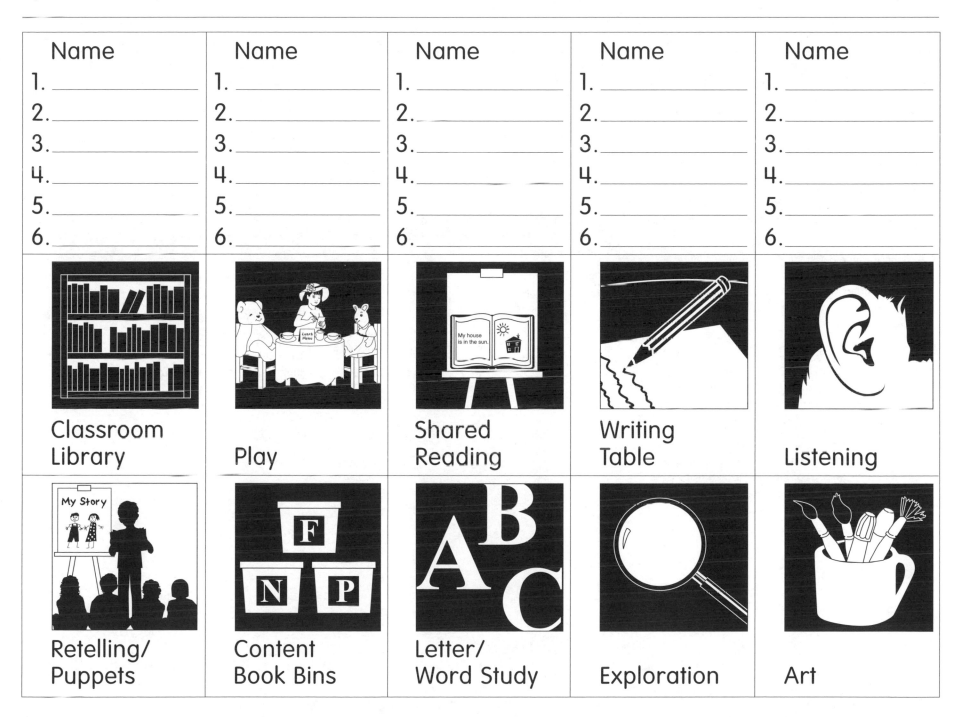

Name	Name	Name	Name	Name
1.	1.	1.	1.	1.
2.	2.	2.	2.	2.
3.	3.	3.	3.	3.
4.	4.	4.	4.	4.
5.	5.	5.	5.	5.
6.	6.	6.	6.	6.
Classroom Library	Play	Shared Reading	Writing Table	Listening
Retelling/ Puppets	Content Book Bins	Letter/ Word Study	Exploration	Art

Differentiating the Support for Individual Children	Differentiating the Materials and Activities	Differentiating the Logistics of Center Use
■ Regardless of the children's age group, be available to provide on-the-spot, individualized support during center time. Preschool teachers should be available during the entire center period. Kindergarten teachers may go back and forth between centers and small groups. First-grade teachers may use most of the center period to work with small groups.	■ Monitor how well the materials and activities are working for the children. Make on-the-spot adaptations and suggestions as appropriate.	■ Regularly monitor how well the environmental and social conditions are supporting children's learning. Make adjustments as appropriate.
■ Meet with some children right as centers begin to provide extra modeling (beyond that which you have done for the class), or to help them get started on an activity.	■ Offer choices of activities, allowing students to differentiate for themselves.	■ Purposefully place a child in a group based on how well he or she will work with the other children in that group.
■ Arrange for an older student or parent volunteer to work with children at certain centers. Volunteers may provide support with instructions, read materials aloud, support children's writing, or take dictation for writing (if assigned by you).	■ Offer choices of learning materials. Ensure that materials reflect a variety of topics, interests, languages, and cultures.	■ Vary the number of students per group. Some children work better in smaller groups.
■ Assign a peer with whom to complete certain activities.	■ Provide reading materials written at varied levels of difficulty, but with similar content. Support children in finding the appropriate material.	■ Offer choices in terms of where to work in the classroom; allow the child to work in a quiet, private, or soft area, with another child if appropriate.
■ For students receiving special services, collaborate with the special needs teacher to arrange for the children to receive support during some center activities.	■ Instead of requiring writing, allow for audio taping, drawing, or sculpting; or arrange for an aide or adult volunteer to take dictation.	■ Provide alternative seating or create standing space.
■ For bilingual or English language learners, arrange for center-based instructional support in the native language. This may involve arranging for an aide or a volunteer adult with whom to read a text, discuss its content, discuss instructions, preview a text, respond to a piece of literature, and so on.	■ For bilingual or English language learners, arrange for students to read, write, listen to, and discuss literature in both languages.	■ Offer a variety of mini-environments in the classroom (peaceful, active, dimly lit, lamp-lit, room for movement, soft music, etc.).
		■ Offer students opportunities to work and speak in their native languages — with other children who speak the same language.

Bibliography of Professional Resources

Afflerbach, P. 2002. "Teaching Reading Self-Assessment Strategies." In Block, CC., and Pressley, M. (eds.), *Comprehension Instruction: Research-Based Best Practices.* New York: The Guilford Press.

Allington, R. 2001, 2006. *What Really Matters for Struggling Readers: Designing Research-Based Programs.* New York: Longman.

Allington, R. 2002. "What I've Learned About Effective Reading Instruction From a Decade of Studying Exemplary Elementary Classroom Teachers." *Phi Delta Kappan.* 83 (10): 740-747.

Anderson, R., Wilson, P., and Fielding, L. 1988. "Growth in reading and how children spend their time outside of school." *Reading Research Quarterly,* 231 (3): 285-303.

Armbruster, B., Lehr, F., and Osborn, J. 2001. *Put Reading First: The Research Building Blocks for Teaching Children to Read.* Center for the Improvement of Early Reading Achievement.

Atwell, N. 2007. *The Reading Zone: How to Help Kids Become Skilled, Passionate, Habitual, Critical Readers.* New York: Scholastic.

Betts, E. 1946. *Foundations of Reading Instruction.* New York: American Book.

Bloodgood, J. 1999. "What's in a name? Children's name writing and literacy acquisition." *Reading Research Quarterly,* 34: 342-367.

Boyd, M. & Rubin, D. 2006. How contingent questioning promotes extended student talk: The function of display questions. *Journal of Literacy Research,* 38 (2), 141-169.

Braunger, J., and Lewis, J. 2006. *Building a Knowledge Base in Reading.* IRA/NCTE.

Bredekamp, S., and C. Copple. 1997. *Developmentally Appropriate Practice in Early Childhood Programs.* Washington DC: National Association for the Education of Young Children.

Bond, G., and Dykstra, R. 1967. The cooperative research program in first-grade reading instruction. *Reading Research Quarterly,* 2: 10-141.

Bruner, J. 1983. Play, thought and language. *Peabody Journal of Education,* 60: 60-69.

Burns, Griffin, and Snow. 1999. *Starting Out Right: A Guide to Promoting Children's Reading Success.* National Academy Press.

Bus, A., van Ijzendoorn, M., and Pellegrini, A. 1995. "Joint Book Reading Makes for Success in Learning to Read: A meta-analysis on intergenerational transmission of literacy." *Review of Educational Research,* 65: 1-21.

Campbell, J., Voelkl, K., and Donahue, P. 1997. *NAEP 1996 trends in academic progress* (NCES Publication No. 97985r). Washington, DC: U.S. Department of Education.

Celano, D., and Neuman, S. 2001. "The Role of Public Libraries in Children's Literacy Development: An Evaluation Report." Pennsylvania Department of Education.

Christen, W., and Murphy, T. 1991. "Increasing Comprehension by Activating Prior Knowledge." ERIC Digest. Identifier: ED328885.

Christie, J., and Enz, B. 1992. "The effects of literacy play interventions on preschoolers' play patterns and literacy development." *Early Education and Development,* 3 (3): 205-220. EJ 447 691.

Cullinan, B. 2000. "Independent Reading and School Achievement." (3) *School Library Media Research.* http://www.ala.org/ala/aasl/aaslpubsandjournals/slmrb/slmrcontents/volume32000/independent.htm

Cullinan, B., and Galda, L. 1998. *Literature and the Child (4th ed.).* New York: Harcourt Brace.

Cunningham, P. 2005. "If they don't read much, how they gonna get good?" *The Reading Teacher,* 59(1):88-90.

DaSilva, K. 2001. "Drawing on Experience: Connecting Art and Language." *Primary Voices K-6,* 10 (2): 2-9.

Dewey, J. 1897. "My Pedagogic Creed." *School Journal* 54 (1): 77-80.

Dudley-Marling, C., and Paugh, P. 2004. *A Classroom Teacher's Guide to Struggling Readers.* Portsmouth, NH: Heinemann.

Duke, N., and Bennett-Armistead, V. 2003. *Reading and writing informational text in the primary grades: Research-based practices.* New York: Scholastic.

Duke, N., and D. Pearson. 2002. *What Research Has to Say About Reading.* International Reading Association.

Egawa, K. (no date) *Writing in the Early Grades.* http://www.ncte.org/prog/writing/research/113328.htm. National Council of Teachers of English.

Ehri, L., and Sweet, J. 1991. "Fingerpoint Reading of Memorized Text: What Enables Beginners to Process the Print." *Reading Research Quarterly.* 26 (4): 442-462.

Elley, W. 1992. *How in the World Do Students Read? The IEA Study of Reading Literacy.* The Hague, Netherlands: International Association for the Evaluation of Educational Achievement.

Ferreiro, E., and A. Teberosky. 1982. *Literacy Before Schooling.* Portsmouth, NH: Heinemann.

Gee, J. 2000. *Discourse and Sociocultural Studies in Reading.* In M.L. Kamil, P.B. Mosenthal, Pearson, P.D. and Barr, R. (eds.), Handbook of Reading Research, Vol. 3: 195-207. New York: Erlbaum.

Gentry, J., and Gillet, J. 1993. *Teaching Kids to Spell,* Portsmouth, NH: Heinemann

Gibson, A., Gold, J., and Sgouros, C. 2003. "The Power of Story Retelling." *The Tutor.* Northwest Regional Laboratory. http://www.nwrel.org/learns/tutor/spr2003/spr2003.html

Gillespie, M. 2005. "Using Research on Writing." *Focus on Basics: Connecting Research and Practice.* National Center for the Study of Adult Learning and Literacy. http://www.ncsall.net/?id=339

Goodman, Y., and Wilde, S. 1992. *Literacy Events in a Community of Young Writers.* New York: Teachers College Press.

Goodman, Y. 1996. "Evaluation of Students: Evaluation of Teachers." In Wilde, S (ed.), *Notes from a Kidwatcher.* 228-241. Portsmouth, NH: Heinemann.

Goodman, Y., Watson, D., and Burke, C. 2005. *Reading Miscue Inventory.* Katonah, New York: Richard C. Owen Publishers.

Graves, D. 1982. *A Case Study Observing the Development of Primary Children's Composing, Spelling,* and Motor Behaviors During the Writing Process, Final report, National Institute of Education-G-78-0174.

Graves, D. 1983. *Writing: Teachers and Children at Work.* Portsmouth, NH: Heinemann.

Griffin, M. 2002. "Why don't you use your finger? Paired reading in first grade." *The Reading Teacher,* 55: 766-774.

Guthrie, J., and Wigfield, A. 2000. "Engagement and motivation in reading." In Kamil, M.L, Mosenthal, P.B., Pearson, P.D., and Barr, R. (eds.), *Handbook of Reading Research,* Vol. 3: 403-422. New York: Erlbaum.

Heard, G. 1989. *For the Good of the Earth and Sun: Teaching Poetry.* Portsmouth, NH: Heinemann.

Hiebert, E. 2004. "The Effects of Text Difficulty on Second Graders' Fluency Development." http://www.textproject.org/library/papers/Hiebert-2004a.pdf

Holdaway, D. 1979. *The Foundations of Literacy.* Portsmouth, NH: Heinemann.

International Reading Association and the National Association for the Education of Young Children (IRA/NAEYC). 1998. "Learning to Read and Write: Developmentally Appropriate Practices for Young Children." A Joint Position Statement. *Young Children* 53 (4): 30-54.

Johnson, J., and J. Christie. 2000. "Draft of the Platform of the Play, Policy, and Practice Caucus." *Play, Policy, & Practice Connections: Newsletter of the Play, Policy, & Practice Caucus of the National Association for the Education of Young Children, IV* (2): 9-11.

Keene, E., and R. Zimmermann. 1997. *Mosaic of Thought: Teaching Comprehension in a Reader's Workshop.* Portsmouth, NH: Heinemann.

Kohl, H. 1999. *A Grain of Poetry: How to Read Contemporary Poems and Make Them a Part of Your Life.* New York: Harperflamingo.

Lonigan, C, and J. Anthony, B. Bloomfield, S. Dyer, and C. Samwel. 1999. "Effects of Two Shared-Reading Interventions on Emergent Literacy Skills of At-Risk Preschoolers." *Journal of Early Intervention,* 22(4) 306-322.

Krashen, S. 1993. *The Power of Reading; Insights from the Research.* Englewood, CO: Libraries Unlimited.

Krashen, S. 1995. "School Libraries, Public Libraries and the NAEP Reading Scores." *School Library Media Quarterly* 23: 235-37.

Kress, G. 1997. *Before Writing: Rethinking the Paths to Literacy.* London: Routledge.

Leipzig, D. 2000. Word Study: A New Approach to Teaching Spelling. *Reading Rockets.* http://www.readingrockets.org/article/80

McGee, L., and Morrow, L. 2005. *Teaching Literacy in Kindergarten.* New York: Guilford.

Meiers, M. 2004. Reading for Pleasure and Literacy Achievement. *Research Developments.* Issue 12. http://www.acer.edu.au/publications/newsletters/resdev/rd12/RD12_reading.html

Meisinger, E., Schwanenflugel, P., Bradley, B., and Stahl, S. 2004. "Interaction Quality During Partner Reading." *Journal of Literacy Research,* 36: 111-140.

Michigan Department of Education. Grade Level Content Expectations: English Language Arts Across the Grades. www.michigan.gov/mde

Morrow, L. 1985. "Retelling Stories: A Strategy for Improving Young Children's Comprehension, Concept of Story Structure, and Oral Language Complexity." *The Elementary School Journal,* 85(5): 646-661.

Morrow, L. 1990. "Preparing the classroom environment to promote literacy during play." *Early Childhood Research Quarterly,* 5 (4): 537-554.

Morrow, L., and Rand, M. 1991. "Preparing the classroom environment to promote literacy during play." *In Play and Early Literacy Development,* Christie, J.F. (ed.), 141-165. Albany: State University of New York.

Mullis, I., Campbell, J., and Farstrup, A. 1993. *NAEP 1992 Reading Report Card for the Nation and the States.* Washington, D.C.: National Center for Education Statistics.

A Position Statement of the International Reading Association and the National Association for the Education of Young Children. 1998. Learning to Read and Write: Developmentally Appropriate Practices for Young Children.

Neuman, S., Copple, C., and Bredekamp, S. 2000. (NAEYC 2000). *Learning to Read and Write: Developmentally Appropriate Practices for Young Children.* Washington, DC: National Education for the Association of Young Children.

NCTE. 2004. *NCTE Beliefs about the teaching of writing.* http://www.ncte.org/about/over/positions/category/write/118876.htm

Opitz, M., and Rasinski, T. 1998. *Good-Bye Round Robin: 25 Effective Oral Reading Strategies.* Portsmouth, NH: Heinemann.

Pellegrini, A., and Galda, L. 1993. "Ten Years After: A Re-examination of Symbolic Play and Literacy Research." *Reading Research Quarterly,* 28: 163-175.

Peterson, R., and Eeds, M. 1990. *Grand Conversations: Literature Groups in Action.* New York: Scholastic.

Piaget, J. 1952. *The Construction of Reality in the Child.* New York: Basic Books.

PISA. 2000. "Engagement Impacts Reading Proficiency." Organization for Economic Cooperation and Development: Program for International Student Assessment. http://www.ncte.org/about/research/articles/110444.htm

Pressley, M. 2001. "Comprehension Instruction: What makes sense now, what might make sense soon." *Reading Online,* 5: (2).

Pressley, M., Allington, R., Wharton-McDonald, R., Block, C. and Morrow, L. 2001. *Learning to Read: Lessons from Exemplary First Grade Classrooms.* New York: Guilford.

Roskos, K., and Christie, J. 2001. "Examining the Play-Literacy Interface: A critical review and future directions." *Journal of Early Childhood Literacy,* 1 (1): 58-89.

Roskos, K., and Neuman, S.B. 1993. "Descriptive observations of adults' facilitation of literacy in young children's play." *Early Childhood Research Quarterly,* 8: 77-97.

Scanlon, D., and Vellutino, F. 1996. "Prerequisite skills, early instruction, and success in first-grade reading: Selected results from a longitudinal study." *Mental Retardation and Development Disabilities Research Reviews,* 2: 54-63.

Schrader, C. 1989. "Written language use within the context of young children's symbolic play." *Early Childhood Research Quarterly,* 4: 225-244.

Snudden, C. 1998. "Shared Reading Motivates Children." *Literacy Today* (15). www.literacytrust.org.uk/Pubs/shared.html

Sulzby, E. 1985. "Kindergartners as Writers and Readers." In *Advances in Writing Research, Vol. 1: Children's Writing Development,* Farr, M., ed., 127-99. Norwood, NJ: Ablex.

Swanson, H., and Hoskyn, M. 1998. "Experimental Intervention Research on Students with Learning Disabilities: a meta-analysis of treatment outcomes." *Review of Educational Research,* 68 (3): 277-321.

Strickland, D., and Shanahan, T. 2004. "Laying the Groundwork for Literacy." *Educational Leadership* 61(6): 74-77.

Taylor, D., and Dorsey Gaines, C. 1988. *Growing Up Literate: Learning from Inner-city Families.* Portsmouth, NH: Heinemann.

Taylor, B. M., Pearson, P. D., Clark, K., and Walpole, S. 2000. "Effective schools and accomplished teachers: Lessons about primary-grade reading instruction in low-income schools." *Elementary School Journal,* 101 (2): 121-165.

Teale, W. 1986. "Home background and young children's literacy development." In *Emergent literacy: Writing and reading.* Teale, W. H., and Sulzby, E., eds., 173-206. Norwood, NJ: Ablex.

Templeton, S. and Morris, D. 2000. "Spelling." In *Handbook of Reading Research, Volume III.* Kamil, M., Mosenthal, P., Pearson, P.D., and Barr, R., eds., 525-543. Mahwah, NJ: Erlbaum.

Villaume, S., and Brabham, E. 2002. "Comprehension Instruction: Beyond Strategies." *The Reading Teacher,* 55 (7): 672-675.

Vukelich, C. 1991. "Materials and modeling: Promoting literacy during play." In *Play and early literacy development,* Christie, J.F. (ed.), 215-231. Albany: State University of New York.

Vukelich, C. 1994. "Effects of play interventions on young children's reading of environmental print." *Early Childhood Research Quarterly,* 9: 153-170.

Vygotsky, L. 1978. *Mind in Society: The Development of Higher Psychological Processes,* Cole, M, John-Steiner, V., Scribner, S., and Souberman, E. (eds). Cambridge, MA: Harvard University Press.

Welsch, J., Sullivan, A., and Justice, L. 2003. "That's my letter!: What preschoolers' name writing representations tell us about emergent literacy knowledge." *Journal of Literacy Research,* National Research Council. http://www.findarticles.com/p/articles/mi_qa3785/is_200307/ai_n9291165/pg_7

Wylie, R., and Durrell, D. 1970. "Teaching Vowels Through Phonograms." *Elementary English* 47: 787-791.

Bibliography of Children's Literature

Adler, David. 1999. *A Picture Book of Amelia Earhart.* New York: Holiday House.

------. 1992. *A Picture Book of Helen Keller.* New York: Scott Foresman.

------. 1990. *A Picture Book of Abraham Lincoln.* New York: Holiday House.

------. 1991. *A Picture Book of Martin Luther King, Jr.* New York: Holiday House.

Allen, Judy. 2002. *Are You an Ant?* New York: Kingfisher.

------. 2003. *Are You a Butterfly?* New York: Kingfisher.

------. 2000. *Are You a Snail?* New York: Kingfisher.

Alvarez, Julia. 2000. *The Secret Footprints.* New York: Alfred A Knopf.

Archambault, John, and Martin, Jr., Bill. 2000. *Chicka Chicka Boom Boom.* New York: Aladdin.

Ashman, Linda. 2003. *Babies on the Go.* San Diego: Harcourt.

Avison, Brigid. 1993. *I Wonder Why I Blink and Other Questions About My Body.* New York: Scholastic.

Baker, Lucy. 1990. *Life in the Rainforests.* New York: Two-Can Publishing.

Bang, Molly. 1999. *When Sophie Gets Angry Really, Really Angry.* New York: Scholastic.

Berger, Melvin. 2001. *Is a Dolphin a Fish?* New York: Scholastic.

Berger, Samantha, and Moreton, Daniel. 1998. *Games.* New York: Scholastic.

Bond, Felicia. 2000. *Tumble Bumble.* New York: HarperTrophy.

Boynton, Sandra. 1982. *Moo, Baa, La La La.* New York: Little Simon.

Brett, Jan. 1999. *Gingerbread Baby.* New York: G.P. Putnam's Sons.

------. 1997. *The Hat.* New York: Putnam.

------. 1989. *The Mitten.* New York: G.P. Putnam's Sons.

------. 2004. *The Umbrella.* New York: Putnam.

Brooks, Felicity. 1990. *Protecting Endangered Species.* London: Usborne.

Brown, Margaret Wise. 2002. *Sailor Boy Jig.* New York: Margaret K. McElderry.

Bruel, Nick. 2005. *Bad Kitty.* New Milford, CT: Roaring Brook Press.

Canizares, Susan, and Chessen, Betsey. 1999. *Two Can Do It!* New York: Scholastic.

Carle, Eric. 1967. *Brown Bear, Brown Bear, What Do You See?* New York: Henry Holt and Company.

------. 2000. *Does a Kangaroo Have a Mother, Too?* New York: HarperCollins.

------. 1987. *Have You Seen My Cat?* New York: Simon & Schuster.

------. 1984. *The Very Busy Spider.* New York: Putnam.

Carlstrom, Nancy White. 1991. *Wild, Wild Sunflower Child,* Anna. New York: Aladdin.

Carter, David, (ill.) 1992. *Over in the Meadow: An Old Counting Rhyme* (Based on the original by Olive A. Wadsworth). New York: Scholastic

Chen, Chih-Yuan. 2004. *Guji Guji.* Kane/Miller.

Cherry, Lynne. 1990. *The Great Kapok Tree.* New York: Harcourt Brace & Co.

-----. 1992. *A River Ran Wild.* New York: Scholastic.

Chessen, Betsey, and Chanko, Pamela. 1999. *Thank You.* New York: Scholastic.

Chessen, Betsey, and Moreton, Daniel. 1999. *Getting Around.* New York: Scholastic.

Cisneros, Sandra. 1997. *Hairs/Pelitos.* New York: Dragonfly (RandomHouse).

Cole, Kristin. 2001. *Edward Degas: Paintings That Dance.* New York: Grossett and Dunlap.

Coles, Robert. 1995. *The Story of Ruby Bridges.* New York: Scholastic.

Cooney, Barbara. 1999. *Eleanor.* New York: Puffin.

-----. 1982. *Miss Rumphius.* New York: Penguin.

Cooper, Elisha. 2002. *Ice Cream.* New York: Greenwillow.

Cooper, Floyd. 1994. *Coming Home: From the Life of Langston Hughes.* New York: Putnam.

Cowley, Joy. 1987. *Just This Once.* San Diego, CA: Wright Group.

-----. 1980. *Mrs. Wishy-Washy.* New York: Philomel.

Crews, Donald. 1991. *Big Mama's.* New York: Trumpet.

-----. 1992. *Shortcut.* New York: HarperChildren's.

Crimi, Carolyn. 2000. *Don't Need Friends.* New York: Random House.

Bibliography of Children's Literature cont.

Cronin, Doreen. 2000. *Click, Clack, Moo: Cows That Type*. New York: Simon & Schuster.

Curtis, Jamie Lee. 1993. *When I Was Little: A Four-Year-Old's Memoir of Her Youth*. New York: Scholastic.

Darling, Kathy. 1996. *Rain Forest Babies*. New York: Walker.

------. 1997. *Desert Babies*. New York: Walker.

Day, Alexandra. 1985. *Good Dog,* Carl! New York: Aladdin.

Degen, Bruce. 1983. *Jamberry*. New York: Harper & Row.

DePaola, Tomie. 1998. *Mice Squeak We Speak.* New York: Scholastic.

Dorros, Arthur. 1995. *Isla*. New York: Dutton.

------. *A Tree is Growing*. 1997. New York: Scholastic.

Edwards, Pamela Duncan. 2002. *Muldoon*. New York: Scholastic

Ehlert, Lois. 1991. *Red Leaf, Yellow Leaf.* Orlando, FL: Harcourt Brace.

Engelbreit, Mary. 2005. *Mary Engelbreit's Mother Goose.* New York: HarperCollins.

Esbensen, Barbara Juster. 2002. *Swing Around the Sun*. Minneapolis, MN: Lerner.

Farris, Cristine King. 2005. *My Brother Martin: A Sister Remembers.* New York: Aladdin.

Fleming, Denise. 1994. *Barnyard Banter.* New York: Henry Holt.

Fox, Mem. 1986. *Hattie and the Fox*. New York: Aladdin.

------. 2005. *Hunwick's Egg.* Orlando, FL: Harcourt.

-----. 1994. *Koala Lou*. Orlando, FL: Harcourt.

------. 1993. *Time for Bed.* Orlando, FL: Harcourt

------. 1994. *Tough Boris.* New York: Harcourt Brace.

Galdone, Paul. 1973. *The Little Red Hen*. New York: Clarion.

-----. 1973. *The Three Billy Goats Gruff.* New York: Clarion.

------. 1994. *The Three Little Pigs.* New York: Clarion.

George, Kristine O'Connell. 1997. *The Great Frog Race and Other Poems*. New York: Houghton Mifflin.

Gibbons, Gail. 2001. *Apples*. New York: Holiday House.

------. 1987. *Dinosaurs*. New York: Holiday House.

------. 2001. *Ducks*. New York: Holiday House.

------. 1988. *Farming*. New York: Holiday House.

------. 1991. *Monarch Butterfly*. New York: Holiday House.

------. 1997. *Pigs*. New York: Scholastic.

------. 1990. *Weather Words*. New York: Holiday House.

Gill, Shelley. 1995. *Swimmer*. Homer, AK: Paws IV Publishing.

Ginsberg, Mirra. 1988. *The Chick and the Duckling.* New York: Aladdin.

Gray, Libba Moore. 1999. *My Mama Had a Dancing Heart*. New York: Orchard.

Grey, Mini. 2005. *Traction Man*. New York: Knopf.

Grimes, Nikki. 1984. *Meet Danitra Brown*. New York: Lothrop, Lee, & Shepard.

Guarino, Deborah. 2004. *Is Your Mama a Llama?* New York: Scholastic.

Halpern, Shari. 1992. *My River*. New York: Scholastic.

Havill, Juanita. 1987. *Jamaica's Find*. New York: Houghton Mifflin.

Hawes, Judy. 2000. *Why Frogs are Wet*. New York: Scholastic.

Heard, Georgia. 1992. *Creatures of Earth, Sea, and Sky*. Honesdale, PA: Boyds Mills/Wordsong.

Heller, Ruth. 1999. *Animals Born Alive and Well*. New York: Putnam.

------. 1981. *Chickens Aren't the Only Ones*. New York: Putnam.

------. 1983. *The Reason for a Flower.* New York: Putnam.

Henkes, Kevin. 1991. *Chrysanthemum*. New York: Greenwillow.

------. 1996. *Lilly's Purple Plastic Purse*. New York: Greenwillow.

------. 1987. *Sheila Rae, The Brave.* New York: Scholastic.

Herrera, Juan Felipe. 2000. *The Upside Down Boy.* San Francisco: Children's Book Press.

Hesse, Karen. 1999. *Come On, Rain!* New York: Scholastic.

Hest, Amy. 2003. *Where's My Hug.* New York: Scholastic.

Himmelman, John. 1990. *Ibis: A True Whale Story.* New York: Scholastic.

Hoban, Tana. 1988. *Look! Look! Look!* New York: Scholastic.

Hoberman, Mary Ann. 1998. *Miss Mary Mack.* New York: Scholastic.

Hodge, Deborah. 1999. *Wild Dogs.* Tonawanda, NY: Kids Can Press.

Hoffman, Mary. 1991. *Amazing Grace.* New York: Dial.

Howard, Elizabeth Fitzgerald. 1991. *Aunt Flossie's Hats (and Crab Cakes Later).* New York: Clarion.

Hudson, Wade. (selected by). 1993. *Pass It On: African American Poetry for Children.* New York: Scholastic.

Hutchins, Pat. 1986. *The Doorbell Rang.* New York: Scholastic.

------. 1971. *Rosie's Walk.* New York: Aladdin.

------. 1974. *The Wind Blew.* New York: Scholastic.

Issa. http://www.toyomasu.com/haiku/#issa

Jenkins, Steve. 1997. *Biggest, Strongest, Fastest.* York: Houghton Mifflin.

Johnson, Angela. 1989. *Tell Me a Story, Mama.* New York: The Trumpet Club.

Juster, Norton. 2005. *The Hello, Goodbye Window.* New York: Hyperion.

Kiuchi, Tatsuro. 1993. *The Lotus Seed.* New York. Harcourt Brace.

Krull, Kathleen. 2003. *Harvesting Hope.* New York: Harcourt.

Lamm, C. Drew. *Sea Lion Roars.* New York: Scholastic.

Lester, Alison. 1996. *When Frank Was Four.* New York: Houghton Mifflin.

Lionni, Leo. 1967. *Frederick.* New York: Alfred A. Knopf.

MacLachlan, Patricia. 1994. *All the Places to Love.* New York: HarperCollins.

Markle, Sandra. 2006. *Army Ants.* Minneapolis: Lerner.

Marshall, James. 1988. *Goldilocks and the Three Bears.* New York: Dial.

Martin, Jr., Bill. 1967. *Brown Bear, Brown Bear, What Do You See?* New York: Henry Holt and Company.

Marzollo, Jean. 1999. *I am a Leaf.* Scholastic.

------. 1998. *Once Upon a Springtime.* New York: Scholastic.

Miranda, Anne. 1997. *To Market, To Market.* New York: Harcourt.

McCloskey, Robert. 1996. *Make Way for Ducklings.* New York: Viking.

McPhail, David. 1997. *Edward and the Pirates.* New York: Scholastic.

Mosel, Arlene. 1968. *Tikki Tikki Tembo.* New York: Holt, Rinehart, and Winston.

Muth, Jon. 2003. *Stone Soup.* New York: Scholastic.

------. 2005. *Zen Shorts.* New York: Scholastic.

Numeroff, Laura. 2004. *Beatrice Doesn't Want To.* New York: Candlewick.

------. 1999. *The Best Mouse Cookie.* New York: HarperCollins.

------. 1998. *If You Give a Pig a Pancake.* New York: Scholastic.

------. 2000. *If You Take a Mouse to the Movies.* New York: Scholastic.

O'Connor, Jane. 2003. *Mary Cassatt: Family Pictures.* New York: Grosset and Dunlap.

Palatini, Margie. 1995. *Piggie Pie.* New York: Scholastic.

Peek, Merle. 1992. *Mary Wore Her Red Dress.* New York: Clarion.

Perez, Amada Irma. 2000. *My Very Own Room.* San Francisco: Children's Book Press.

Pinkney, Sandra L. 2000. *Shades of Black: A Celebration of Our Children.* New York: Scholastic.

Piper, W. 2005. *The Little Engine that Could.* New York: Philomel.

Polacco, P. 1992. *Mrs. Katz and Tush.* New York: Bantam.

------. 1992. *Chicken Sunday.* New York: Scholastic.

Pomerantz, Charlotte. 1989. *The Chalk Doll.* New York: Lippincott.

Prelutsky, J. *If Not for the Cat.* 2004. New York: HarperCollins.

Raffi. 1999. *Down By the Bay.* New York: Crown.

Rand, Gloria. 1992. *Prince William*. New York: Henry Holt and Co.

Rappaport, Doreen. 2001. *Martin's Big Words*. New York: Hyperion.

Riley, Linea Asplind. 1997. *Mouse Mess*. New York: Blue Sky Press.

Ringgold, Faith. 2003. *If a Bus Could Talk: The Story of Rosa Parks*. New York: Aladdin.

Root, Phyllis. 2001. *One Duck Stuck*. Cambridge, MA: Candlewick Press.

Rosen, Michael. 2003. *We're Going on a Bear Hunt*. New York: Aladdin.

Rosetti, Christina. *Who Has Seen the Wind?* http://celtic.benderweb.net/cr/cr81.html

Rotner, Shelley. 2002. *Pick Me an Apple!: From Seed to Tree*. New York: Scholastic.

Royston, Angela. 1991. *What's Inside? My Body*. New York: Scholastic.

Rucki, Ani. *When the Earth Wakes*. 1998. New York: Scholastic.

Ryder, Joanne. 1988. *The Snail's Spell*. New York: Puffin.

------. 2003. *Wild Birds*. New York: HarperCollins.

Rylant, Cynthia. 1996. *An Angel for Solomon Singer*. New York: Scholastic.

------. 2000. *In November*. New York: Harcourt.

------. 1991. *Night in the Country*. New York: Aladdin.

------. 1996. *The Old Woman Who Named Things*. New York: Harcourt.

------. 1982. *When I Was Young in the Mountains*. New York: Dutton.

------. 1993. *The Relatives Came*. New York: Aladdin.

Sayre, April. 2005. *The Bumblebee Queen*. Watertown, MA: Charlesbridge.

Schart Hyman, Tina. 1987. *Little Red Riding Hood*. New York: Holiday House.

Schreiber, Anne. 1994. *Boots*. New York: Scholastic.

------. 1994. *Log Hotel*. New York: Scholastic.

Sendak, Maurice. 1988. *Where the Wild Things Are*. New York: HarperCollins.

Shannon, David. 1998. *No, David!* New York: Scholastic.

------. 2006. *Good Boy, Fergus*. New York: Scholastic.

Shaw, Nancy E. 1997. *Sheep in a Shop*. New York: Houghton Mifflin.

------. 1992. *Sheep on a Ship*. New York: Houghton Mifflin.

Sherrow, Victoria. 1994. *Chipmunk at Hollow Tree Lane*. New York: Scholastic.

Shore, Diane and Jessica Alexander. 2006. *This is the Dream*. New York: HarperCollins.

Simont, Marc. 2001. *The Stray Dog*. New York: Scholastic.

Singer, Marilyn. 2003. *Fireflies at Midnight*. New York: Atheneum.

Soto, Gary. 1993. *Too Many Tamales*. New York: Putnam & Grossett.

Steig, W. 2003. *When Everybody Wore a Hat*. New York: HarperCollins.

Steptoe, John. 1997. *Creativity*. New York: Clarion.

------. 1987. *Mufaro's Beautiful Daughters*. New York: William Morrow & Company.

Stevens, Janet. 1995. *Tops and Bottoms*. Orlando, FL: Harcourt Brace & Company.

Tomecek, Steve. 2002. *Dirt*. Washington, DC: National Geographic Society.

Trapani, Iza, (ill.). 1993. T*he Itsy Bitsy Spider*. Watertown, MA: Charlesbridge.

Van Frankenhuyzen, Robbyn Smith. 2001. *Adopted by an Owl: The True Story of Jackson the Owl*. Chelsea, MI: Sleeping Bear Press.

------. 2004. *Saving Samantha*. Chelsea, MI: Sleeping Bear Press.

Wahl, J. 2004. *Knock! Knock!* New York: Henry Holt and Company.

Ward, Cindy. 1997. *Cookie's Week*. New York: Putnam.

Wells, Rosemary. 1998. *The Bear Went Over the Mountain*. New York: Scholastic.

------.1997. *McDuff Comes Home*. New York: Hyperion.

------. 1997. *McDuff Moves In*. New York: Hyperion.

Whybrow, Ian. 2004. *The Noisy Way to Bed*. New York: Arthur A. Levine.

Widman, Christine. 1991. *The Lemon Drop Jar*. New York: Simon & Schuster.

Wild, Margaret. *Our Granny*. Boston: Houghton Mifflin.

Wildsmith, Brian. 1974. *Squirrels*. Oxford: Oxford University Press.

Willems, Mo. 2004. *The Pigeon Finds a Hot Dog!* New York: Scholastic.

Williams, Laura. 2006. *The Best Winds*. Honesdale, PA: Boyds Mills.

Williams, Linda. 2002. *Horse in the Pigpen*. New York: HarperCollins.

Williams, Sue. 1989. *I Went Walking*. New York: Harcourt.

Winkelman, Barbara. 1999. *Flying Squirrel at Acorn Place*. New York. Scholastic.

Winter, Jeanette. 1992. *Follow the Drinking Gourd*. New York: Knopf.

Winter, Jonah. 2002. *Frida*. New York: Arthur A. Levine.

Wood, Audrey. 1982. *I'm as Quick as a Cricket*. Swindon, England: Child's Play International.

------. 1994. *Silly Sally*. New York: Harcourt.

------. 1998. *The Little Mouse, the Red Ripe Strawberry and the Big Hungry Bear.* Swindon, England: Child's Play International.

------. 1984. *The Napping House*. New York: Harcourt.

Woodson, Jacqueline. 2001. *The Other Side*. New York: Putnam.

Yolen, Jane. 1987. *Owl Moon*. New York: Philomel.

Young, Ed. 2006. *My Mei Mei*. New York: Philomel.

Zelinsky, Paul O. 1986. *Rumplestiltskin*. New York: Dutton.

Zoehfeld, Kathleen Weidner. 1994. *Dolphin's First Day: The Story of a Bottlenose Dolphin*. Norwalk, CT: Trudy Corporation